Father Damien...

"A Bit of Taro, A Piece of Fish, and A Glass of Water"

Anwei Skinsnes Law
Henry G. Law

IDEA Center for the Voices of Humanity

Library of Congress Control Number: 2009925671
ISBN 978-0-9802123-1-0

Cover Photo: Father Damien at Kalawao. *Photo by Dr. Eduard Arning, c. 1884.*
Hawaiian Historical Society and Museum für Völkerkunde Hamburg

Back Cover Photo: Joseph Manu in 1933. *Damien Museum Archives*

Dedicated to Richard Marks

Whose impact on the history of Kalaupapa is as
immeasurable as his love for Father Damien

Contents

Foreword

About 15 years before I became the first native-born Bishop of Honolulu, I discovered an untold story about my great-grandfather, John Santos, and his daughter, my great aunt, Minnie Santos Arruda. They had been sent to Kalaupapa on the island of Molokai because they were suspected of having leprosy. This was a family story I had never heard until I was well into middle age. When I became Bishop of Honolulu in 2005, I mentioned this untold story in the *Hawaii Catholic Herald*. My cousins, who had lived in Hawaii all their lives, were surprised to know that their own relatives had had leprosy.

For generations, the story of the men, women and children who had leprosy in Hawaii was largely untold, although the memories of those sent to Kalaupapa were vivid in the minds and hearts of their loved ones. Stories of Father Damien, Mother Marianne and others who went to bring comfort and hope to the people of Kalaupapa abounded, but were mostly told by those living outside the settlement. King Kalakaua, Queen Kapiolani, Robert Louis Stevenson and others sang their praises in speeches and print media. But, the voices of the people who were sent to Kalaupapa have been largely absent from written history. Even though they wrote hundreds of letters and petitions and provided eye-witness testimony to the historical events of the 19th and 20th centuries, their perspective simply hasn't been included in traditional histories.

This very inspiring book, filled with the words and recollections of the people of Kalaupapa who knew Father Damien personally, not only sings his praises but reveals a great deal about the struggles and joys they experienced. This is a book about Father Damien De Veuster, SS.CC., the Belgian Sacred Hearts missionary who was ordained a priest at the Cathedral of Our Lady of Peace in Honolulu; who worked tirelessly to share the love of Christ on the Big Island of Hawaii; and who volunteered to serve forever the people of Kalaupapa, who had been taken so far from home and family in order that society might be protected. He only served in Kalaupapa for 16 years until his death, as a person affected by leprosy, in 1889. But, with his canonization as a Saint of the Catholic Church in 2009, he stands as a perpetual reminder of the need for compassion and justice as society faces new challenges that seek to divide and separate God's children.

As we listen to these simple but beautiful stories of the friendship between Father Damien and the people of Kalaupapa, may we learn to leave no story untold. May we learn the importance of all human beings as we refer to them not as a disease but as people afflicted with a disease, yet people who bring us hope and light in spite of all their challenges. And may we learn from Father Damien that one's own story becomes much more fascinating and much more meaningful when it is focused on others.

-- The Most Reverend Clarence (Larry) Silva
    Bishop of The Catholic Diocese of Honolulu

At Kalaupapa, Bishop Silva views the gravestone of his great-grandfather, John Santos, which has been dislocated from the grave. *Photo by Wayne Levin*

History, as anything else, is seen and understood by where a person stands on the mountain.

All people climb the same mountain. The mountain, however, has many pathways -- each with a different view. A person knows and understands only what he sees from his own pathway, and as he moves, his view will change. Only when he reaches the top of the mountain will he see and understand all the views of mankind. But who among us has reached the top of the mountain? Tomorrow, we too will see a different view. We have not finished growing. [1]

Kaili`ohe Kame`ekua, of Kamalo, Molokai, a *kaula*, "true light carrier," who knew Father Damien and lived to be 115 years old, as told in oral history and published in *Tales from the Night Rainbow*

Introduction

David Kamahana, who met Father Damien in 1888. *Courtesy John Cambra*

The story of Father Damien has been told and retold hundreds of times in books and articles. However, these accounts have generally not included the voices and insights of the people who were most affected by Father Damien's presence, the people who lived and worked alongside him at Kalaupapa. Nor have previous accounts included the words and feelings of his parishioners on the Big Island of Hawaii and in other parts of the island of Molokai.

By choosing a pathway that highlights these previously unheard voices, it is hoped that this book will enable our knowledge and understanding of Father Damien to gain new depth, to become more complete. At the same time, including the voices of the people who actually lived the history that is being told leaves less room for misinterpretation. When people's voices are included, they are able to define themselves rather than be limited by the imagination and perceptions of others who did not know them. Most important, including the voices of the people whom Father Damien counted as his friends adds great warmth, simplicity and humanity.

Joseph Manu, a resident of Pelekunu Valley, Molokai, who later contracted leprosy, was close friends with Father Damien for 16 years, from the time Father Damien first arrived at Kalaupapa in 1873 until his death in 1889. At the age of 81, Joseph Manu provided testimony for the Cause of Father Damien and observed: "I can in all truth say that nobody knew Father Damien better than I during the 16 years prior to his death." He reflected on Father Damien's prayerfulness and how he was a simple man who was satisfied with "a bit of taro, a piece of fish, and a glass of water."[2]

Kaili`ohe Kame`ekua lived at Kamalo, Molokai, for most of her life. Believing that it was important for future generations to "know the truth about who and what they were," she passed down her wisdom and knowledge through oral history prior to her death in 1931 at the age of 115. Included in that oral history were her recollections of how she and others would watch Father Damien come "riding along on his donkey" and also how the people of Kamalo helped him to build St. Joseph's Church in 1876.[3]

Ambrose Hutchison was the son of Maria Moa, a Hawaiian woman from Maui, and her husband, Dr. Ferdinand Hutchison, the Scottish-born President of Hawaii's Board of Health who selected the Makanalua peninsula (commonly known as Kalaupapa) as the site of isolation for people with leprosy. Sent to Kalaupapa in 1879 because he had leprosy, Ambrose Hutchison would reside there for 53 years, working closely with Father Damien for ten years and assuming major leadership roles. Ambrose Hutchison's name is only briefly mentioned in traditional histories, if he is mentioned at all. His memoirs, compiled shortly before his death, provide unique insights into Father Damien, the man whom he described as his "true friend in word as well as in deed."[4]

Two 12-year-old girls, Pohaku Melemai and Malie Kauluwela arrived at Kalaupapa on November 13, 1888, on the same ship with Mother Marianne Cope, Sister Leopoldina Burns and Sister Vincentia McCormick. Together with the other girls residing at the Bishop Home for Girls, Pohaku Melemai and Malie Kauluwela attended Father Damien's funeral. Almost 50 years later, they both vividly remembered wearing black sashes that Mother Marianne had made for all of the girls the night before.[5]

Referring to herself as Father Damien's "daughter in spirit,"[6] Mele Meheula was sent to Kalaupapa in 1888 as a nine-year-old girl and lived there until her death in 1957. A most important link between Father Damien and the people who were sent to Kalaupapa long after his death, Mele Meheula and her friends made wreaths for Father Damien the day before his body was removed from Kalawao in 1936 and returned to Belgium.

In 2008, some 120 years after her father, David Kamahana, was sent to Kalaupapa as a teenager, Emma Kamahana Dickerson recalled his words: "He said that he knew Father Damien and liked him because he taught him how to love and how to have patience."[7] Other Kalaupapa residents who knew Father Damien personally and lived long enough to be witnesses for the Cause of Father Damien included David Ilihia and John Puaina Wilmington.

By looking at the 16 years of his life spent at Kalaupapa through the eyes of those who knew him best, this book will focus on Father Damien's love, his patience and his fervent belief in justice. It is these characteristics that have endeared him to modern day generations at Kalaupapa, people who never knew him personally but have always been inspired and comforted by his legacy. At the same time, anyone who has been closely associated with Kalaupapa well understands that while the people of Kalaupapa have been inspired by Father Damien, he was, in turn, most certainly inspired by the people of Kalaupapa who had lost everything, yet still had so much to give. This book is ultimately the story of that relationship.

Authors' Notes: Diacritical marks in current use to aid in the pronunciation, spelling and comprehension of Hawaiian words are not generally used in this book for names and quotes from the time period before these marks were in common practice. However, they are retained in quotations from modern sources (i.e., Tales from the Night Rainbow) or in the names of individuals who used them.

The background "fabric" that appears in the chapter headings is adapted from the fabric used in the sling that Father Damien wore in the last months of his life, as seen in the photo on page 89.

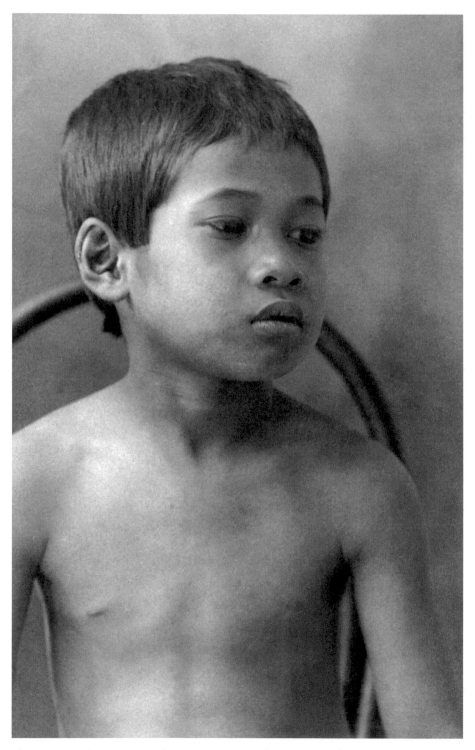

Akiona Peter Akim, sent to Kalaupapa as a young boy in 1900, about 12 years after Peter Camacho. *Hawai'i State Archives*

Christmas, 1888

I send this short note to you because we sent some Christmas presents to our child Peter Camacho to be under your care and that you will open the box yourself and give it to him whatever it contains. A tin of crackers and some toys for him to play with to amuse himself . . . we send our greetings to you and to our child Peter, our beloved child, and tell him he should not forget to pray to God. Dear Father Damien, I am very grateful to you for the care of my child in the strange land without any hope for our seeing him again in this world. So Father good-bye for the present and tell Peter that we all send our love and greetings to him from his brother and sisters. Tell him that they did never forget him for a moment from the day he left Honolulu till this moment.[8]

Francisco Camacho to Father Damien, December 16, 1888, regarding his nine-year-old son, Peter Camacho, who had been sent to Kalaupapa earlier that year

In fulfillment of my duties as priest, being in daily contact with the distressed people, I have seen and closely observed the bad effect of forcible separation of the married companions. It gives them an oppression of mind which, in many instances, is more unbearable than the pains and agonies of the disease itself.[9]

Father Damien, March 11, 1886

Chapter 1

An Oppression of Mind

Resident of Kalaupapa.
Damien Museum Archives

When Father Damien arrived at Kalaupapa on May 10, 1873, some 924 people had been separated from their families and isolated on this remote peninsula because they had leprosy. Between his arrival and his death on April 15, 1889, another 2,835 people would be taken from everything they held dear and sent to Kalaupapa on the premise that society needed to be protected at all costs.[10]

The isolation of people with leprosy in Hawaii began on January 6, 1866, when the first eight men and four women were put on board the schooner *Warwick* bound for Kalaupapa. With them were at least four family members, including a small boy whom they hid in their midst.[11] These family members were the first in a long line of *mea kokua*, people who helped, people who comforted, people who refused to allow those who were sick to be sent away alone.

From the very beginning, the Hawaiian people simply could not accept the idea that sickness was justification for separation. In what might be termed non-violent resistance today, family members often hid their relatives at home as long as possible and also sought to accompany family members to Kalaupapa as *mea kokua* (helpers). The isolation laws were simply not consistent with the values of the Hawaiian culture.

The Makanalua peninsula, commonly referred to as Kalaupapa. *Photo by A. Law*

Waialeia Valley

Waihanau Valley

Pelekunu Valley

Waikolu Valley

Kalawao

Makanalua

Kalaupapa

The different land divisions of the peninsula, along with adjacent valleys. *Photo by Henry Law*

Individuals being transported by small boat from an inter-island steamer to the Kalaupapa landing, early 1900's. *Hawai'i State Archives*

Some of the *kamaaina*, original residents, of Kalaupapa. *Photo by Dr. Eduard Arning, c. 1884. Hawaiian Historical Society and Museum für Völkerkunde Hamburg*

In later years, William Malo reflected on his family's love and the cultural values that led to trying to keep those who were sick at home: "The Hawaiians were neighborly, loving each other and helping each other in times of need and suddenly a different kind of lifestyle was thrust on them --'Me first' -- it was just not the way they behaved. To the Hawaiian people, it was always *Nui ke aloha mamua o ka maka'u* -- great love over fear."[12] This belief was also illustrated by the *kamaaina*, the original residents of the peninsula, many of whom refused to give up their land and be relocated elsewhere. Instead, they chose to stay and help support their new neighbors in any way that they could.

In his report to the Legislature of 1868, Dr. Ferdinand Hutchison, President of the Board of Health, stated that the primary goal was "to exterminate the disease" even if it meant depriving people of "the ordinary rights of citizens."[13] The Hawaiian people simply did not believe that having a disease was grounds for losing your rights or your family.

Less than two weeks before Father Damien arrived at Kalaupapa, Jonathan Napela accepted the position of Resident Superintendent at Kalaupapa in order to allow him to accompany wife, Kiki, to Kalaupapa. Jonathan Napela was a former judge and a prominent member of the Mormon Church who, together with George Q. Cannon, translated the Book of Mormon into Hawaiian. He expressed the views common amongst many of the Hawaiian people who strongly believed that the laws of God were greater than the laws of man.

Jonathan Napela contracted leprosy five years after arriving at Kalaupapa and died shortly thereafter. *Photograph by Charles R. Savage, c. 1869. BYU-Hawai`i Archives*

I do humbly petition the Board of Health in their kindly parental affection to consent that I live with my wedded wife, as a kokua.

On the 3rd day of August, 1843, I took my woman to live with me as wedded wife. On this day I swore before God to care for the wife in time of health and in sickness, and that only death would separate us.[14]

Ambrose Hutchison would later describe Jonathan Napela and Father Damien as "the best of friends." Although they were members of different religions and different cultures they respected each other and shared a common understanding of the devastating effect that the isolation policy had on people. Father Damien wrote: "I think it is but justice, and in accordance with Divine and humane law, that faithful husbands and wives . . . should be allowed to accompany their partners to their exile in Kalawao."[15] Father Damien added that the *mea kokua* were of "great help and assistance" to individuals and were also "of great value to the local administration for carrying on all work needed for the welfare of the place."

In his report to the Board of Health in 1886, Father Damien further commented:

> *In the fulfillment of my duties as priest, being in daily contact with the distressed people, I have seen and closely observed the bad effect of forcible separation of the married companions. It gives them an oppression of mind which, in many instances, is more unbearable than the pains and agonies of the disease itself. This uneasiness of the mind is, in the course of time partly forgotten by those unfortunates only, who throw themselves into a reckless and immoral habit of living. Whereas, if married men or women arrive here in company with their lawful mates they accept at once their fate with resignation, and very soon make themselves at home in their exile.*[16]

A draft of Father Damien's report, "A Personal Experience," written in 1886, in which he described the "oppression of mind" he observed when husbands and wives were separated. *Hawai'i State Archives*

Father Damien understood the loneliness of being separated forever from those you loved. Upon leaving Belgium, he wrote to his family: "We are in the hands of God . . . Good bye, dearest parents, henceforward we shall not have the happiness of seeing one another, but we shall always be united by that tender love which we bear to one another . . ."[17]

In his memoirs, Ambrose Hutchison recalled how Father Damien would tell him about his boyhood and early life during "moments of leisure" when they would sit and chat in Father Damien's parlor. He recalled Father Damien's great love for his family:

> . . . in talking to me about them, his inward feeling of affection would overcome him and he was silent for some moments. Naturally during that moment of silence I felt and shared the same feeling of love with the kind tender hearted priest. Dear Father Damien. It is the common heritage of all people to cherish the memory and love of those whom they hold dear in life.

. . . you could not wish for better people; gentle, pleasant-mannered, exceedingly tender-hearted, they neither seek to amass riches, or live in luxury, or dress much, but are most hospitable, and ready to deprive themselves of necessaries in order to supply your every want if you have to ask a night's shelter from them . . . I like them immensely . . .[18]

Father Damien, 1864

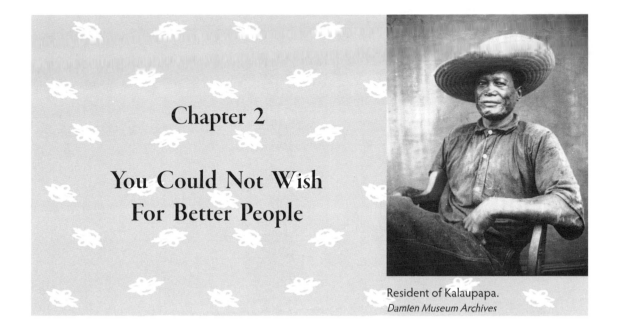

Chapter 2

You Could Not Wish For Better People

Resident of Kalaupapa.
Damien Museum Archives

Brother Damien De Veuster had arrived in Honolulu on March 19, 1864, following a difficult voyage from Belgium. After being ordained at Our Lady of Peace Cathedral in Honolulu, he spent two months on Oahu and then proceeded to the Big Island of Hawaii, where he spent the next nine years working with the people in the parishes of Puna, Kohala and Hamakua. Ambrose Hutchison described Father Damien's first mission in Hawaii:

The young newly ordained priest whom we shall know by name Father Damien was sent to Puna, Island of Hawaii, a large rough country District without a resident priest He took passage on a schooner bound for Hawaii ports and landed at Kapoho, a village where there was a church and Mission house for a priest residence. His arrival was an occasion for the villagers and members of the church to welcome him, and bringing him food and things they deemed he needed. This show of kindness gave Father Damien his first taste of the natives hospitality that impressed him and above all else the satisfaction of a large attendance at the first Mass said by him in the village church of Kapoho, and the beginning of his missionary labor among the natives on the Island of Hawaii. On that occasion he regretted, as the Father relates, his ignorance of the language of the natives to preach and [he] expressed in words to them his heart's intent ... To speak and talk the native language to succeed in his mission work spurred him to study hard to master it.

Father Damien wrote about some of his first impressions to his parents:

> *You must not be surprised, my dear father, that our natives here use neither spoons nor forks, neither tables nor chairs. It is the custom to eat with their fingers, and to sit on the ground: but they have nice mats in their houses to sit on. It is the same thing in the church. At first I made benches for them, but they would not use them, and I find it much more economical.*[19]

Ambrose Hutchison noted that Father Damien was "not permanent in one place -- more of a traveling priest than a resident one" and described his travels and the hospitality he received along the way:

> *From Puna Father Damien was sent to Kona . . . he labored among the natives of South and North Kona, Kohala and Hamakua Districts. He traveled on horseback throughout these four Districts taking him about three weeks to make the round journey before he is back to his headquarters . . . Wherever he is received on his traveling tour he accepted native hospitality . . .*

On the Big Island, Father Damien also became aware of the separation of families due to the isolation policies related to leprosy. Ambrose Hutchison recalled:

> *During the years of his travels throughout the Kona, Kohala and Hamakua Districts as a Missionary among the natives . . . Father Damien had seen much sorrow among native families. The arrest of suspects and alleged leprous persons, either a father or mother, son or daughter or some other dear relative by Police Officers and led away like criminals and cast into lockups awaiting for a vessel to take them to the living grave of Kalawao, on the Island of Molokai, where they never hoped to see the dear ones left behind in this life. These scenes made Father Damien's heart bleed for these unfortunate people . . .*

In 1870, Father Damien wrote to Dr. Ferdinand Hutchison, requesting permission for a man to visit family members at Kalawao.[20] In April, 1873, shortly before he left for the island of Maui to join Bishop Louis Maigret and several other priests for the dedication of St. Anthony's Church, Father Damien described his feelings:

By order of the Board of Health all the leprosy victims they could collect have been sent to the Settlement on Molokai, as to a government prison. Many of our Christians from at Kohala also had to go. I can only attribute to God an undeniable feeling that soon I shall join them. However, eight years of service among Christians you love and who love you have tied us by powerful bonds. Even just joking about my going to Molokai upsets them . . .[21]

Years after leaving the Big Island, Father Damien would still receive letters from his former parishioners. Michael Kaloa recalled the day he left: "We still remember when you left us. Everyone could not hold the tears back for they realized that a true friend will depart and never to return. You consoled us in our troubles and made us new people again."[22]

As they gathered together on Maui, Bishop Maigret and Fathers McGinnis, Damien, Boniface, Gulstan, Gregory, Rupert, Aubert and Leonor, discussed the Catholic Mission's responsibility to the Catholics on the Island of Molokai, especially those isolated at Kalawao.[23] A Protestant church, Siloama, had been organized by some of the first people sent to Kalaupapa in 1866 and a church building had been constructed in 1871. A Catholic priest from Maui or Oahu would occasionally travel to Molokai and in 1872 Brother Victorin Bertrand built a wooden chapel in Honolulu and transported it to Kalawao, where it was blessed on May 30 and dedicated to St. Philomena.

When the subject of Kalawao was discussed on Maui, it was suggested that Fathers Damien, Gulstan, Boniface and Rupert take turns residing at the Settlement. They would serve on a rotating basis, each spending three months at Kalawao and the remainder of the year at their parishes on Hawaii and Maui. The Bishop agreed and Father Damien offered to be the first to go.

Bishop Maigret and Father Damien arrived at Kalaupapa on board the steamer *Kilauea*, together with 36 men and women who had leprosy. A number of these individuals were from the Big Island of Hawaii including a man named Kainoa from Kohala, the location of Father Damien's former parish.[24] According to Bishop Maigret's diary, they visited the hospital at Kalawao and then entered "the humble chapel" recently built by Brother Bertrand. The

Bishop noted that the people came to the church in "impressive enough numbers." He added: "I speak a few words to them -- they seem happy to see us -- Fr. Damien will remain some 2 weeks among them -- a petition bearing 200 signatures is presented to us – they are asking that a priest remain permanently among them, but where is one to be found . . ."[25]

Father Damien in 1873, the year he went to Kalaupapa. He was 33 years old.
Damien Museum Archives

Within two days, Father Damien had decided that he wanted to stay permanently. On May 12, the steamer *Warwick* arrived from Honolulu with another 17 people who had leprosy. One of the new arrivals was John Upa, "a leading spirit," who had served as a guide for visitors to the volcano on the Big Island of Hawaii.[26] That same day, Father Damien wrote to his Superior, Father Modeste, indicating his desire to remain at Kalawao:

> *I am sending you these words by way of the schooner Warwick to let you know that from now on there should be a resident priest in this post. The sick arrive by boatloads, and they die as a consequence. I am living under a Puuhala (that is to say, a pandanus tree) while waiting for the lumber to build a house such as you would consider appropriate. Send me a case of wine, some spiritual books and others for studying, some shirts, trousers, shoes, the bell, rosaries, catechisms, altar bread, small and large, a bag of flour, and a lockbox. Please write to Rev. Father Gulstan to have him take charge of Kohala until my return there, unless you find one of the Kona fathers to take charge permanently. You know my intention . . .[27]*

Close to 500 families were separated in 1873, more than in any other single year, as a result of the Government's heightened efforts to enforce the isolation of people with leprosy.[28] In March, Rudolph Meyer, Agent for the Board of Health on upper Molokai, had indicated that there was room for 100 more people at Kalawao and an additional 100 if the lands of the *kamaaina* at Kalaupapa were purchased.[29] In the next three months, more than 300 people were sent to the Settlement, and no *mea kokua* were allowed to accompany them. Housing was inadequate and food now had to be provided for more than 800 people.

Father Damien later described the people who were at the Settlement when he arrived: "Some of them were old acquaintances of mine from Hawaii, where I was previously stationed . . . to the majority I was a stranger."[30] He observed that most of the people who had leprosy were living at Kalawao and were only allowed to go to the Kalaupapa landing place when a ship arrived. About 80 individuals were living in the hospital, while the others "had taken their abode further up towards the valley." He further commented:

They had cut down the old pandanus, or puuhala groves, to build their houses, though a great many had nothing but branches of castor oil trees with which to construct their small shelters. These frail frames were covered with ki leaves . . . or with sugar-cane leaves -- the best ones with pili grass. I myself was sheltered during several months under the single pandanus tree . . . Under such primitive roofs were living pell-mell, without distinction of ages or sex, old or new cases, all more or less strangers one to another . . . They passed their time with playing cards, hula (native dances), drinking fermented ki-root beer, home-made alcohol, and with the sequels of all this. Their clothes were far from being clean and decent on account of the scarcity of water, which had to be brought at that time from a great distance . . . [31]

Ambrose Hutchison described Father Damien's early days at Kalawao and the tree that provided him shelter before he built his house: "This Puhala tree and spot was dear to the heart of Father Damien as the kind sheltering friend of those first eventfull weeks of his mission . . ."

The pandanus tree under which Father Damien slept is to the right of the Church. The section with the steeple was built by Father Damien, probably in 1876-1877. *Detail of photo by Dr. Eduard Arning, c. 1884. Hawaiian Historical Society and Museum für Völkerkunde Hamburg*

Joseph Manu first met Father Damien shortly after his arrival, when Manu was about 16 years old and would bring food from Pelekunu Valley to Kalawao, which was about two miles away. Joseph Manu recalled that it took some people time to accept Father Damien: ". . . in the beginning people mistrusted him, but bit by bit they started to trust him and love him for his great love."

In later years, Joseph Dutton described how Father Damien would make it a point to greet new arrivals at Kalaupapa: "He was very hospitable. He made a practice of meeting the weekly steamers at Kalaupapa . . . For a long time, the steamer arrived very early in the morning, and, in order to reach the landing in time, he used to say his Mass, on those mornings, at about four o'clock. So he was the foremost, or among the foremost, in meeting any passengers that were being landed . . ."[32]

Richard Marks, who was sent to Kalaupapa in 1956, heard about Father Damien from the "old-timers" who recalled that:

> *He treated them as they would be expected to be treated by their own families. Because those who had known him on the Big Island turned to him for help, the others began to notice what he was trying to do. They began to accept him because of who he was. He was accepted because he was a simple man. Damien was more down-to-earth, more like the Hawaiians . . . He proved himself by the touching of the hands. I've heard the old timers say that -- just the touch . . .*[33]

Ambrose Hutchison described how about two weeks after Father Damien's arrival, the schooner *Warwick* arrived with lumber for the Catholic Mission and "by the kind attention of Mr. Napela, then superintendent . . . the lumber was loaded on ox-carts and taken to the mission ground at Kalawao." Hutchison noted that when the lumber arrived, Father Damien immediately "cast off his cassock," donned a "denim frock" and began to work on his residence with the help of a *kokua*. Hutchison continued: "In six weeks the building was completed, painted inside and out, and ready for use. Father Damien moved in and was at home." Father Damien wrote to his family that the "hut" he built for himself was 16 feet long and 10 feet wide. Hutchison also commented that while he was building his house, Father Damien "never neglected his priestly duties, visiting the sick and dying . . ." If an immediate call came, he would drop his tools, change from his work clothes into his cassock and with stole in hand he "hastened to the dying to administer the last rites of the church."

In 1874, Father Damien wrote to his family that he had built a church in another part of Molokai, at Kaluaaha:

> *During the summer, I went to another part of this island, where I remained four months in the character of a carpenter, putting up a new church, 44 feet long, 22 wide; with 10 Gothic windows, and a tower 50 feet high . . .*

> *These ten years I have been on the Mission, I have built a church or chapel every year. The habit I had at home of practising different kinds of work, is of immense use to me here.*[34]

Ambrose Hutchison described Father Damien's carpentry skills when, a few years later, he enlarged the church at Kalawao.

> *Father Damien again donned his work clothes and with his helper started work on the addition to the chapel in accordance with his plan, and [after] some weeks of steady daily work Father Damien had the satisfaction of seeing the carpenter work on the exterior of the new building with its tall steeple pointed skyward completed . . .*

> *They continued to work steadily for some weeks longer to finish what carpentering work remained undone. With the carpenter work finished in good workmanship, in every detail the handy work of a master mechanic. Painters applied paint on the finished wood work in and out in varied hue with finishing touches of colors here and there . . . the beautifull little church was ready for dedication to the services of God which the village of Kalawao was fortunate to have in its midst.*

> *From then on the ringing of the church bell every Sunday and Holy days of obligation, vibrating joyously on its lofty rest place, heard throughout the village of Kalawao*

calling the faithful to attend Mass and the ringing of the Angelus, morning, noon and evening every day in the year was constant reminder ... that their Saviour and dearest friend liveth and is ever here in that little wonder house of worship, ready through the intercession of His holy mother to lift and lighten the burdens of those heavily laden.

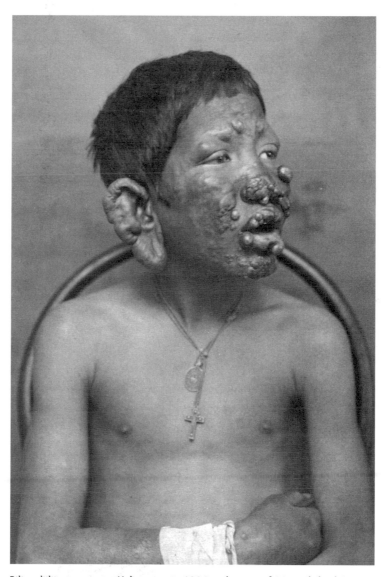

Pilipo Iiilii was sent to Kalaupapa in 1896 at the age of 11, and died 8 years later. *Hawai'i State Archives*

It is a Melencolly sight to see the poor Sick with Sunken Eyes look at you and when asked how they fare reply, "We're hungry"... On the 15th of last Month, two men died from Hunger... The man Kealohi died on the 23rd and "a little poi" were his dieing words. [35]

Peter Kaeo, one of 477 people sent to Kalaupapa in 1873

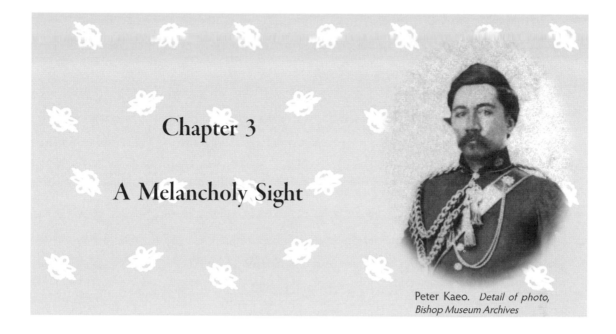

Chapter 3

A Melancholy Sight

Peter Kaeo. *Detail of photo, Bishop Museum Archives*

An important eye-witness to the living conditions at Kalaupapa in 1873 and 1874 was Peter Young Kaeo, a former member of the House of Nobles, who was sent to Kalaupapa on June 30, 1873. He described the situation in detail to his cousin, Queen Emma, in a series of letters. In addition to providing descriptions of the difficult situation that faced people with regard to food and living conditions, Peter Kaeo's letters also revealed the overwhelming loneliness felt by those who had been taken so far from home, no matter what their social status. Upon arriving at Kalaupapa, he wrote to Queen Emma:

> *I have arrived safe . . . I wished I could come to you once more and repeat the sad word 'Good Bye' -- but no . . . 'Home' -- I will not dwell on this sad subject for It might be tiresome to you, but to me it is comfort to think of the past and the future . . .*[36]

Peter Kaeo described how he and Jonathan Napela, the Resident Superintendent, would ride around the peninsula to survey the situation of the people. On one occasion, they came across three men, three women and a boy about five or six years old, living in a large cave.

> *Oh you cannot form any Idea how they looked . . . Napela asked them whether they had anything to eat, and they answered that they had sufficient enough to last them till*

Wednesday, which is the day the Poi is served. Napela also asked them why they did not
go to the Hospital, and they replied that their Cave was more preferable to the Hospital,
as the Hospital was "Anu Anu" [very cold].[37]

In response to Queen Emma's wish to send $30 to help people who were in need of clothing, Peter Kaeo wrote that at least half of the people were in need of clothing. He noted that they were in dread of the coming rainy season because their blankets were threadbare, women had no undergarments, and their children were dressed in rags.[38]

In a report written in 1886, Father Damien described similar scenes of how when he arrived the people were "in general very destitute of warm clothing."

The Settlement being situated at the northern side of the island, and backed at the south
by very high and steep mountains, the climate is naturally cool. The winter season
brings forth generally a long spell of cold weather…

Those who have suitable and warm clothes to protect themselves from the inclemency of
the weather resist it generally very well, but for those who, through neglect or destitution,
have barely enough to cover their nakedness, the cold and damp weather has a bad
effect. They then begin to feel feverish and cough badly; swelling in the face and limbs
sets in, and if not speedily attended to the disease generally settles in the lungs, and thus
hastens them on the road to an early grave.[39]

An indication of the hardship faced by people was also seen in Jonathan Napela's first letter from Kalawao stating that he had bought some property belonging to the late William Uwelealea Humphreys, a former Representative of the Legislature of the Hawaiian Kingdom,[40] who had been sent to Kalawao in 1868. The property included a cow, two chairs, a water barrel and washtub. In justifying these purchases to the Board of Health, Napela noted that the cow was a good bargain and that the office had no chairs. The greatest indication of the tremendous hardship faced by the people was Napela's explanation for spending $8.62 on the water barrel and tub: " . . . the water barrel and tub were filled with rain water which is water the sick people can use."[41]

In his 1886 report, Father Damien noted that when he arrived there was a scarcity of water and people had to carry their water in oil cans for a great distance, which made it very hard to keep themselves and their clothing clean. He noted that in the summer of 1873, they received some water pipes and everyone well enough to help willingly laid the pipes and built a small reservoir. Father Damien also described the lack of medical care:

> *I remember well that the poor people were without any medicines, with the exception of a few physics and their own native medicines, from which, I judged, it had been the same from the inauguration of the Settlement. It was a common sight to see people going around with fearful ulcers, which for the want of a few rags, or a piece of lint and a little salve, were left exposed to dirt, flies, and vermin. Not only their sores were neglected, but anyone getting a fever, diarrhea or any other of the numerous ailments … was carried off for want of some simple medicine.* [42]

Father Damien went on to write about William Williamson, a British man who arrived at Kalaupapa in July, 1873. Williamson, who was himself affected by leprosy, had been an assistant to the doctors at Kalihi Hospital. Father Damien recalled:

> *He had quite a practical knowledge of simple medicine, and having been put in charge of our hospital, he especially attended to the patients there, while I for my part, attended largely to those living outside. Our stock of medicine, the greatest part of which was always supplied by the Board, consisted of the most common necessities. Very soon, the people perceiving that by the use of such simple medicines as we had to dispose of, their troubles were greatly ameliorated, and therefore they begun to call more and more for the simple remedies, and thus gradually a perceptible improvement took place. As we had no doctor … we tried to do the best we could.* [43]

Ambrose Hutchison noted that after the *kamaaina*, the original residents, had departed from the Kalawao side of the peninsula, the people who were "left to themselves cut loose from the loved dear ones at home without hope of ever seeing them again, settled down to play a new role in the drama of life . . . There was much suffering . . . The injustice and want of charity, unjust treatment and neglect; this loud complaint some how reached the Government."

In April, 1874, King Kalakaua and Queen Kapiolani visited Kalaupapa. The ascendancy of King Kalakaua to the throne just two months earlier ushered in a new era that would come to be characterized by a deep concern for the people of Kalaupapa. The *Pacific Commercial Advertiser* reported that a crowd of 200-300 people greeted the King and Queen at the Kalaupapa wharf along with the band, which included a drum, fife and two flutes. The report continued:

> *The King and Queen landed at 12:30 and were received by the assembled patients with hearty cheers. The King made a short but feeling address . . . After a few words of kindly recognition to personal acquaintances, and a general "aloha oukou," their Majesties returned to the steamer, painfully affected with the sights of human affliction that they had witnessed.*[44]

That same year, the people of Kalawao sent a petition to the Hawaiian Legislature in which they described their situation and asked for justice.

> *This land is not suitable for us . . . The last months and the first three months of the year are extremely horrible. There is much rain, wind, rough seas and cold. The next six months are terribly hot. It is this cold and heat which carries, overcomes, causes to appear and spread the disease among us which is the cause of our quick death…*
>
> *The insufficiency of food at times. It's true that the taro, sweet potato and other plants have been the customary and useful food to the Hawaiian people since the beginning of the world. You have your health and we are sick. As we have eaten for weeks at a time, or a month or more, only rice and sugar. Poi, the usual food for the Hawaiian people, has been meager. Rice is consumed at one time and poi is consumed at another time and because of this irregularity, the stomachs of the healthy people are askew. Because our stomachs are upset, there is pain and constipation. And there is diarrhea at times. Due to this variety of diet, some people have died…*[45]

Father Damien described how many people lived in damp huts and how a great number of these were blown down during a winter storm in 1874. Peter Kaeo wrote about the effects of that storm to Queen Emma: "Twenty-two Houses were blown down flat to the ground, and 50 more were so damaged that nothing was left but the frame . . . Whole groves of newly planted Bananas were blown down . . . everything that the Natives had planted were more or less damaged . . . Homes which once held a Family of 5 or 6 Tenants were now chackes [shacks]."[46]

While Peter Kaeo described the gravity of the situation to Queen Emma, Father Damien notified someone whom he referred to as "our sympathizing agent." Soon, several schooner loads of timber arrived. Private and charitable sources provided shingles and flooring. Father Damien noted that people who had a little money would build their own houses or hire carpenters, while he and some of the young men built houses for those who could not afford to hire help.[47]

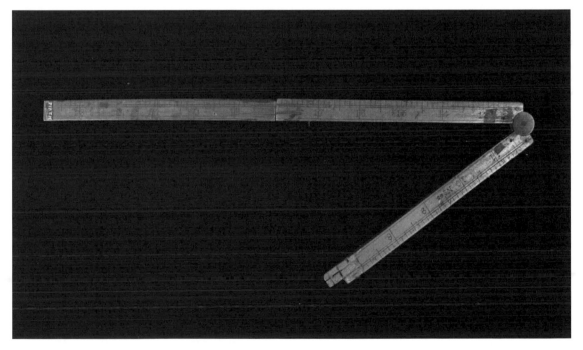

The ruler Father Damien used in his carpentry work. *Wisconsin Historical Society*

In 1877, Father Damien wrote to his mother and brothers: "During the winter I worked hard to enlarge my church and build a pretty tower. Manual work is very good for my health, and I feel well and happy among my unfortunate sick people . . . the Government is ever adding to the number, so that the more we bury the more are sent to us. They are here for the rest of their life . . ."[48] In the same letter, he also noted that he had been to Honolulu and had assisted at the burial of Prince Leleiohoku, the younger brother of King Kalakaua.

When a Special Sanitary Committee, including Walter Murray Gibson, W.O. Smith, and Joseph Nawahi, visited Kalawao in 1878, the issue of digging graves was raised. Kaluakini, a 35-year-old man who had been sent to Kalaupapa in about 1871, testified that if someone refused to help dig a grave, they were denied food rations for the week by the current administration. This statement was confirmed by both Father Damien and Jonathan Napela, who was no longer in charge of the Settlement. Father Damien added that although a man had been hired to dig graves, sometimes two or three people died in one day so extra help was needed.[49] In order to help alleviate the difficulties, they established two funeral associations and three other associations which provided an organized way for individuals to help each other.[50]

After the visit by the Special Sanitary Committee in 1878, the Legislature passed a large appropriation for the Settlement and many comfortable houses were erected and other conditions also improved. Father Damien recalled that these improvements produced a significant change in morale. He also observed that the granting of marriage licenses between those who had leprosy brought about a "great moral improvement."[51]

However, the shortage of food, and in particular *poi*, would continue into the 20th century. As a witness for the Cause of Father Damien, David Ilihia recalled how Father Damien helped make up for shortages in food and other necessities: "He used to go around and visit patients and ask them what they needed. He took notes in his booklet. The day after he brought them the things they wanted."[52]

Sometimes people would send notes to Father Damien, asking for assistance. N. D. Kahoana wrote: "I am asking of you, Damien, our Spiritual Father, to help me to get a wick for the lamp as I have none . . ."[53] M. Leo wrote from Kalaupapa:

Good Father, please see the Superintendent . . . and ask him to furnish a new boat for bringing the freight from the steamer to the landing. The old boat was wrecked and there is [not] anything that the natives can do now . . . The captain of the steamer will not send its boat to the landing for fear of the breakers. Only the old timers know where to come in. There were times that we could not get our food stuff from the steamer and now our boat was wrecked. I am afraid that we take this matter very seriously. Best regards and good luck.[54]

Father Damien also received requests from outside the Settlement. A resident of Pelekunu Valley, P. Nauka, wrote:

Dear Beloved Father Damien. Kindly send me the following: 12 pounds 8-penny nails, 5 pounds 4-penny nails, 2 pieces 1 x 4 x 20. The two pieces of lumber are for the roof of the house. The house is almost complete except for a little part of the roof. I am sorry that the lumber you sent on the Mokolii did not reach here. In sending goods to me, please mark them with my initials P. N.[55]

Pohaku Melemai, who was sent to Kalaupapa in 1888 as a young girl, remembered: "He loved everyone. He was everything for everyone. He was just and loyal with everyone . . . He was impartial with all without exceptions." John Puaina Wilmington, who arrived at Kalaupapa the year before Father Damien died, recalled:

His charity to non-Catholics was just as large as towards his own people and I have seen myself that Calvinists went to Father's house to ask for chickens, eggs, tobacco, sugar, etc. and Father gave freely to them as he gave to Catholics. He was always pleasant and willing to help and did not show displeasure when people did not thank him. Steamers in those days came only once in two or three weeks and sometimes the supply of crackers or bread or rice would run short. Father Damien always kept a little provision of those necessities and gave freely to all who asked . . . "If we need anything," they used to say, "we will go to Kamiano [Damien] and he will help us." The well-to-do . . . lived at Makanalua, a few miles away from Kalawao. The poor dwelled near Father Damien . . .[56]

31

Father Damien used to come to our house in Pelekunu. When we asked him if he wanted something special to eat, he answered: "Do not disturb yourself, I will eat what you have." He was satisfied with a bit of taro, a piece of fish, and a glass of water.

Joseph Manu, Father Damien's close friend for 16 years, whose family lived in Pelekunu Valley, about two miles from Kalawao

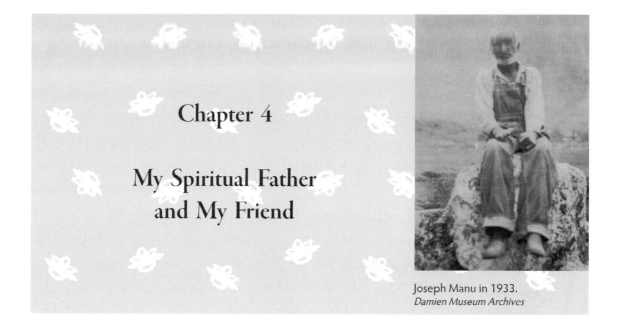

Chapter 4

My Spiritual Father and My Friend

Joseph Manu in 1933.
Damien Museum Archives

Joseph Manu met Father Damien in 1873 when he was about 16 years old. At the age of 81, some 49 years after Father Damien's death, Joseph Manu described his friend's simple lifestyle and great devotion to God and the people of Kalawao.

I was baptized by Bishop Louis Maigret. I am poor. I own only a horse. I have been living in the settlement for 45 years as a patient. Yes, I was here when he landed with the Bishop ... I have known him very well for 16 years ... He didn't like being praised. In the beginning people stayed away from him and were afraid of him because they thought he was severe, but later they lost any fear and loved him. I heard talking about him and also my mother and my father used to talk about him. People spoke well of Father Damien before and after his death due to his benevolence to all ...

Father Damien was fair and honest ... He was fair with Catholics, with Protestants and with all the persons he cared for ... I never heard him talking about his suffering or complaining about the disease. He was a man of will and of strong character. In spite of the pain in his fingers, he worked with the boys and others tilling the land ... He rebuked people who drank alcohol. When somebody was drunk, he rebuked him, sent him home and told him to sleep. He tried to ban drinking from the settlement.

During the 16 years I knew Father Damien, I never noticed anything to reproach him about regarding impurity or immorality. In these matters he was very rigorous with himself and with others. He tried his best to regularize the situation of people living in adultery. His relation with women was very cautious. Not only the population of Kalawao but also of my village Pelekunu considered him a man of exemplary morals … I can in all truth say that nobody knew Father Damien better than me during the 16 years prior to his death …

I used to accompany Father Damien during his apostolic work. I was taking food from Pelekunu to the settlement and there I met Father Damien … Pelekunu was a small village … in a valley of Molokai island, about two miles from Kalawao. You could reach it only by boat … I used to take Father Damien by boat to Pelekunu where he stayed for two or three days. After that, I took him by the same boat to Wailau, distant one mile and stayed there more or less one day or two; from there I took him to Halawa, another valley distant three miles. I left Father Damien in Halawa. From Halawa church he walked to Kaluaaha, distant seven miles. Here he stayed one or two days. Then he walked from Kaluaaha to Kamalo, distant two and a half miles where he stayed one day. During these visits he celebrated Holy Mass, catechized the population and administered the Sacrament. At the end of his ministry in Kamalo he returned, walking to Kalawao, seven miles distant. To do so he had to go down from a steep hill, 2,000 feet high.

Sometimes in his missionary trips the sea became rough and dangerous and I, as his boatman, used to advise Father Damien not to embark until the sea would calm down. Father Damien answered me, "We leave anyway." He never went into the boat without praying …

He was poor but he never complained about it. Father Damien used to come to our house in Pelekunu. When we asked him if he wanted something special to eat, he answered: "Do not disturb yourself, I will eat what you have." He was satisfied with a bit of taro, a piece of fish, and a glass of water. He never wasted food nor would he see others waste it. I and others of my family helped Father Damien as he was poor. We gave him food

High surf, Waikolu Valley. *Photo by Henry Law*

Waikolu Valley, the first valley to the west of Kalawao. *Adapted from photo, Hawai`i State Archives*

Pelekunu Valley. *Adapted from photo, Hawai`i State Archives*

as we knew he was in need. He didn't eat too much, but cooked taro, the principal food of the Hawaiians. Sometimes I asked Father Damien, "Is the food enough?" He answered, "Even too much! Look I have some taro and some fish." I sometimes said to the Father to throw something away as it was old. He answered, "No, it is still good for me." Father Damien warmed up his food a few times to make another meal rather than throw anything away.

Father Damien prayed very often. Often I saw him pray... He called the boys to pray, showing them how to pray. Before entering in my boat he used to recite a prayer and when we were near landing to another bank, the first thing he did was kneel and pray. When he arrived at my house where he used to stay when in Pelekunu, he prayed again. He used to celebrate Mass in my house until he built a small chapel. In the beginning there were only eight Catholics coming to Mass, but very early he converted half of the population and built a chapel. I was his altar boy and I noticed he said Mass slowly and with devotion...

He had a lot of trust in God and in spite of his difficulties he did not lose courage or trust. He tried to encourage the patients to have hope in God...

I have a great affection and love for him as he was my spiritual father and my friend. Every night I pray to Father Damien for his help and his assistance.

Our Lady of Seven Sorrows Church, Kaluaaha, Molokai, which was originally built by Father Damien and the residents of Kaluaaha in 1874.
Photos by Wayne Levin

St. Joseph's Church, Kamalo, Molokai. *Photo by Wayne Levin*

When Father Damien came riding along on his donkey and wanted to talk to us, we were happy to see him. We fed him and gave him a place to rest. I told him I already knew about Jesus and loved him very much. That made him very happy . . . Father Damien wanted to build a hale pule (house of prayer). We promised to help him build such a house.[57]

Kaili`ohe Kame`ekua, who was about 60 years old when St. Joseph's Church was built by Father Damien and the people of Kamalo in 1876

Chapter 5

A Bowl of Perfect Light

Kaili'ohe Kame'ekua was born in 1816 and lived to be 115 years old. Recognized in her youth as a *kaula*, "a true light carrier," her words continue to guide and inspire people of many religions today.[58] Her descriptions of Father Damien, told as oral history within the context of the Hawaiian culture and beliefs he sought to understand, provide unique insights into his relationship with the people he visited regularly who lived outside of Kalaupapa, in other parts of the island of Molokai.

> *Each child born has at birth, a Bowl of perfect Light. If he tends his Light it will grow in strength and he can do all things -- swim with the sharks, fly with the birds, know and understand all things. If, however, he becomes envious or jealous, he drops a stone into his Bowl of Light and some of the Light goes out. Light and the stone cannot hold the same space. If he continues to put stones in the Bowl of Light, the Light will go out and he will become a stone. A stone does not grow, nor does it move . . .*

> *We, on Moloka'i, believed in the light. We tried to keep our bowls full of pure energy and to light the paths of all who came our way . . . When the missionaries came they showed us pictures of Jesus. He was surrounded by light. The stories they told us from their Bible Book were full of loving one another. So, we all became Christians. I became a Christian*

many times. I found that I was also pa'a (locked into my past). I continued to go to the halau [school]; to meditate and spend hours in meditation. I could see nothing wrong in trying to keep my bowl full of light . . .

Jesus was a lover. He taught love. All the stories they told about Him were about love. He taught the same things we taught our children; don't kick unless you expect to be kicked back. Don't say mean things for words hurt worse than stones. Love the old ones, love your parents, love your sisters and brothers, love the babies. The more love you give the more you will receive back into your life.

The missionaries didn't always listen to the things Jesus said. The rules they made and lived by did not come from Jesus. They did not come from the Bible. The rules came from their own minds and hearts . . . I tried to live like they wanted me to live. Many times I could not understand but they were older than I, they were the teachers -- I was the student. I respected them. I covered my body, I did not drink of the 'awa root, I didn't play in the surf on Sabbath but sat listening to sermons all day. I gave up many things that to me were pleasurable. I did not understand many of their laws, but I kept my questions to myself . . .

Father Damien was a quiet man who never yelled at us, or seemed to get angry at us. He asked us questions about why we believed certain things. We loved him. We all wanted him to stay with us but he always got on his donkey and rode away. He explained that Jesus never had a home or a bed, and, like Jesus, he would travel from place to place telling people about the love our heavenly father had for us. Watching him I learned about Jesus. They both were alone. No one took care of them. They had no 'Ohana . . .

One day the teachers at the school and church at Kalua'aha heard that Father Damien had been coming to visit us, and that we were building a hale pule for him. Several of our family who had been "sprinkled" were summoned to Kalua'aha at once. The fathers and mothers at the Mission Station were very angry with us. They said he was not of love, but of darkness. They said his long coat covered a tail, and his hat covered horns. We were all very shocked. We walked home slowly talking about this problem.

Maka wehiwehi had taught me truth was always the same -- yesterday, today and tomorrow. What had been truth hundreds of years ago would still be true hundreds of years in the future. Now, I was being told things that confused me. They all carried the Bible Book. They all told stories of God's love and Jesus. They all believed in prayer houses and meeting on the Sabbath and keeping the day holy. Yet -- one now said the other was not of light but of darkness. By the time we reached home our decision was made. When Father Damien came, we would just lift up the dress (coat) and check . . . If there was no tail, if there were no horns, we would know that he was of the light and we would continue to build for him his hale pule.

When Father Damien came the next time, there was great excitement, for even the youngest children had heard, and were anxious to see what was beneath the robe he wore. Before we had a chance to explain to him what had happened the children rushed forward and pulled up his robe . . . We were all satisfied. The stone belonged to those who would have us believe in such nonsense, and the matter was closed. Father Damien had a congregation.

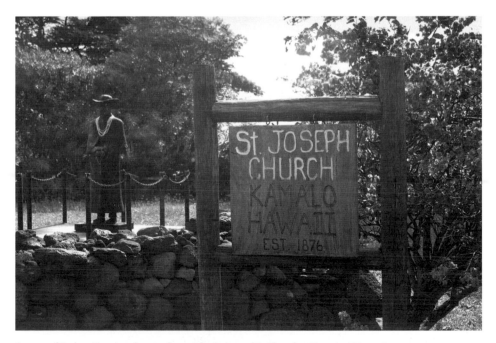

Statue of Father Damien, located outside St. Joseph's Church. *Photo by Wayne Levin*

According to *Tales from the Night Rainbow:*

> *Members of St. Joseph were very active participants in working at the settlement of Kalaupapa. Many made the long journey down to help during the week, returning home on week-ends. They made special foods to be taken to the elderly and the sick. They made a special food for Father Damien that he liked very much called "cookies."*

The grave of Kaili`ohe Kame`ekua in the cemetery of St. Joseph's Church. *Photo by Wayne Levin*

The statue of Father Damien that stands alongside St. Joseph's Church in Kamalo. *Photo by Wayne Levin*

He walked joustily across the yard and through the gate on to the road and up to where I stood. In Hawaiian he greeted, Aloha maikai oe. I reciprocated Aloha maikai oe e ka Makua . . . we stood talking familiarily like old friends for a while . . . He walked away, I looking after him, consciously impressed. I muttered to myself, here is another found friend . . . to know Father Damien intimately was to honor and esteem his worth as a true friend in word as well as in deed.

Ambrose Hutchison, describing his first meeting with Father Damien

Father Damien at Kalawao, c. 1878. *Detail of photo, Hawai'i State Archives*

Chapter 6

Like Old Friends

Ambrose Hutchison was listed as number 2001 in the Kalaupapa Admission Register.[59] Arriving on January 5, 1879, as a young man of 20, he would go on to become highly respected as a steady, consistent and influential leader. He would occupy the position of Resident Superintendent for a total of more than ten years, longer than any other individual who was also dealing with the physical and social effects of leprosy. In his memoirs and reflections on Father Damien and other priests who worked at Kalaupapa, Ambrose Hutchison described his first days at Kalaupapa. His experiences provide important insights into what it was like to find oneself "taken from all a man holds dear in life by force of the law." Upon arriving at Kalaupapa, Ambrose Hutchison first met Father André Burgerman, who worked on the Kalaupapa side of the peninsula. Hutchison recalled:

> *When the Steamer anchored we entered a row boat in company with the two officials and rowed to the Kalaupapa Landing and [were] put ashore and received by the local officials of the settlement. After our names, ages and places we hailed from were taken down, we were left on the rocky shore without food and shelter…*
>
> *I was taken in by a kinsman of my mother who lived at Makanalua who sent a man with a saddled horse to bring me to him. On the way in tow of my guide, as we reached*

the village, a priest came out of a house that stood near the road, partly surrounded by a stone wall on one side and a picket fence on the other (front) side. He walked briskly, passed through the gate on to the road and came out as I approached to pass on my way. Seeing me a stranger he stopped short and in Hawaiian greeted, "Aloha maikai oe." I checked the horse and reciprocated "Aloha maikai oe e ka Makua." He asked if I had eaten? "Not since leaving Honolulu," said I. "Alight and follow me to the house and have a cup of coffee." He turned around and walked back to the house, I following him . . .

In a few minutes coffee was brewed. He put food on the table with steaming coffee, its aroma wafted to the nostrils, and keened the appetite of a hungry man . . . From the bottom of my heart I asked God's blessing for the food which my good unexpected kind friend had placed before me. Never had food tasted so sweet as that I ate on that day, forty eight years ago.

The priest's name was Andre Burgerman, generally known as Father Andrew, a tall lanky man of noble countenance, parish priest, who labored among the kamaainas (old time residents) and others living in Kalaupapa and Makanalua.

The day following his arrival, Hutchison made his way to Kalawao "taking in the sights of scenic view of the surrounding towering precipices and valleys beyond with its long coast line, and the sea surging against this stupendous massive wall of land . . ." This was when he first met Father Damien.

I leisurely went along till I reached the west south corner side of a picket fence surrounding a group of houses (about 12 in number) . . . This was the Hospital that sheltered the sick outcasts, men and women . . . there appeared on the scene a priest who had made his round of visits of the inmates of the institution, a well knit, stocky man of medium height, dark hair, prominent straight thick nose, plump smooth face and wearing gold rim spectacles, garbed in black cassock with a rope girdle of the same color around his waist. On his head a black stiff brim hat held by four bands on the crown.

Kalawao coast. *Photo by Wayne Levin*

The hospital compound, located on the Kalawao side of the peninsula, c.1884. *Hawai'i State Archives*

The road where Ambrose Hutchison first met Father Damien. The Kalawao store can be seen on the right. The hospital compound is behind the fence on the left. *Detail of photo, Courtesy Clarence Coelho*

His right hand held the curved end of stout cane and the other hand held his folded stola. He walked joustily across the yard and through the gate on to the road and up to where I stood. In Hawaiian he greeted, Aloha maikai oe. I reciprocated Aloha maikai oe e ka Makua. He asked my name, where I came from and with whom I lived. Answering his queries, we stood talking familiarily like old friends for a while. Before going, [he] invited me to call on him at his residence which I did later. He walked away, I looking after him, consciously impressed...

My first call on Father Damien at his home in Kalawao some time after meeting him on the road... was on my return from Waikolu (Valley) where I and other fellow unfortunates had gone in the morning to receive our food rations... I found the kind hearted Father at home, he received me cordially like an old friend. I passed a pleasant hour's chat and lunched with him. Thus began an acquaintance which in the course of time, followed by other friendly calls, grew into... [a] lasting friendship...

There was nothing supernatural about Father Damien. He was a vigorous, forceful and impellent man with a big kindly heart in the prime of life and a jack of all trades, carpenter, mason, baker, farmer, medico and nurse, grave digger... He was that type of man of action, bull headed, strong will high minded... of determined tenacity to attain results of his aspiration, but of kindly disposition toward all who came into contact with him... Father Damien's relations with non Catholic Christians were amiable and friendly and especially is this relation true of him and Rev. Hanaloa, Pastor of the congregationalist church of Kalawao...

I have had differences and clashes with him and parted in heat as we could not agree upon a given point of action from the angle of our respective views. When we met again he would say I hope I have not offended you, you have not taken it keenly to heart have you. And when I answered in the negative our difference is ended there and then and we get along very well as though nothing has happened. I loved to work with him in his crusade to put down evil... There was no hypocrisy about him.

For 10 years, Ambrose Hutchison and Father Damien worked closely together, particularly when Hutchison became Resident Superintendent of the Settlement in 1884. In his 1886 report, Father Damien talked about their attempts to curtail "another source of immorality" -- intoxication.

> *There grows very abundantly along the foot of the mountains a plant which the natives call "ki" . . . the root of which, when cooked, fermented, and distilled, gives a highly intoxicating liquid. The process of distilling being very crude and imperfect, produces, naturally enough, a liquor which is totally unfit for drinking. A short time after my arrival the distilling of this horrible liquid was carried on to a great extent. Those natives who fell under the influence of it would forget all decency, and run about in a nude condition, acting as if they were totally mad.* [60]

Ambrose Hutchison described how the situation people were placed in caused many problems with regarding to drinking and disruption of the peace:

> *The existing of making and drinking of intoxicating beverages in a community of isolated people taken from their homes and from every District in the major Islands of the Hawaiian group, and dumped together, left to shift for themselves, without authoritative machinery of law and order to preserve peace, was a menacing factor to the peace and orderly conduct of people . . . Father Damien's intensive lone drive to dry up and stop the drinking . . . met with scant success and satisfaction under three successive superintendents . . . but that did not discourage him . . . He was a holy terror to evil doers whom he had on the run. When they see him coming, they'll scatter to come together at some other favorite place to continue carousing.*

Ambrose Hutchison recalled how, on a daily round to survey the situation at Kalawao, he and Father Damien came upon a man operating a still "of crude construction."

> *[Father Damien] came out holding up to view a white glass bottle filled with clear liquid, saying "here is proof," and poured a little of the liquid in a spoon and touched it with a lighted match that gave a blue flame and consumed it clean, a test that okolehao*

was pure liquor. I received this bottle with its contents from the moonshiner who gave it
to me while I was with him. I have had it in my possession for about six (6) years. The
still from which the liquor came was destroyed. The man promised Father Damien not
to manufacture any more okolehao and kept his promise...

Father Damien and Ambrose Hutchison also made it a point to welcome those who had been taken by force of law from all they held dear. This partnership was evident in a description by Dr. A.A. Mouritz, physician at Kalaupapa from 1884-1887, of a cold rainy night in January, 1885.

In our winter months when the north wind prevails, accompanied with driving rain,
the temperature falls on Molokai as low as 58° F.; this condition of the weather,
together with the thin and scanty clothing generally worn by the inhabitants of
Hawaii, makes a sick person feel cold, and is liable to induce pneumonia.

On one such night, with similar weather conditions described above, there arrived
at Kalaupapa about midnight the steamer "Mokolii" with freight, and about forty
... passengers. There was a heavy surf breaking, the wind was from the North, and
a driving, chilly rain was falling. If it were not for the able handling of the small
boats by the Hawaiian seamen (among the best in the world), they would have been
swamped, overturned and broken to pieces on the rocky shore. By a miracle, none of
these disasters occurred, and both freight and passengers landed in safety, the latter
drenched to the skin by rain and sea.[61]

Dr. Mouritz further noted that although no advance warning had been given regarding the arrival of this ship and its passengers, "the officials were not caught unprepared, both Father Damien and Mr. Ambrose Hutchison had steaming hot coffee and warm food for all who were landed."

I am not a relative by marriage or blood, but I am his daughter in spirit . . . He was an excellent man. I think he was a holy man . . . He showed his great love by taking care of orphans . . . I know this because I was one of them.

Mele Meheula, who was sent to Kalaupapa in 1888 at the age of nine

Chapter 7

Taken Away by Force of Law

Young girl at Kalaupapa. *Detail of photo, A. Law Collection*

When people were sent to Kalaupapa, they lost everything. People who had worked and supported themselves and their families found themselves impoverished. Children who had parents living were labeled "orphans" when they arrived alone at Kalaupapa. Ambrose Hutchison described how boys and girls were "taken away by force of the laws of the Realm from their homes and relatives." Upon arrival at Kalawao, there was no home provided for them and they would sometimes be taken in by those who were very sick and required to "serve as domestics, to look after the horses, go after rations of food, go out and gather wood . . . cook and other menial work."

Father Damien "realized the necessity of a home for boys and old age men and a home for unprotected women and girls" and sought assistance, particularly from Bishop Maigret who, according to Hutchison, "was very solicitous to render every help to Father Damien . . ."

Father Damien's appeal for help was granted and [he] received a load of lumber brought by the transport schooner Warwick and delivered at Kalaupapa and the same brought in oxcart teams to the mission ground at Kalawao. This was about the middle part of the year 1879. With the lumber on the ground Father Damien with a helper started work framing the first building of his contemplated home, a dormitory to accommodate about 12 boys and a kitchen. The foundation of the dormitory was laid down 40 ft. away on the West side of Father Damien's house … the cook house for the boys in the rear North side some 10 ft. away from the dormitory. When the buildings were built and finished and ready for business, the home was opened and 8 boys of different ages, who formerly lived with friends were admitted in the new permanent home built for them and other of their like to follow.

With this small beginning and start, the numbers of inmates admitted to the new home gradually increased [and] that caused Father Damien to build a new and larger dormitory (20 x 40 ft.) in the rear, North side, about 60 ft. away from his house to accommodate comfortably his increasing charges. The home under the charge and direct supervision of Father Damien was showing satisfactory results of much good to the friendless boys and men. They were a happy and contented lot. His keen personal interest in the welfare of his charges had much to do with it.

Father Damien in front of the buildings that appear to be the dormitories for the boys and girls. *Detail of photo by Dr. Eduard Arning, c. 1884, Hawaiian Historical Society and Museum für Völkerkunde Hamburg*

Ambrose Hutchison described how Father Damien interested the boys in farming, a healthy exercise which also "kept them from mischief." They joined in the work "with a will," clearing the land, planting sweet potatoes, onions, cabbage and bananas. They would plant their vegetables and fruit in the large area across the road from the church that would later become the Baldwin Home for Boys. Hutchison noted that when they had a good crop of potatoes, Father Damien would divide the boys' rations. Half would take their ration of *pai ai,* which was pounded into *poi,* the staple of the Hawaiian diet. The other half would take cash in lieu of a bundle of *pai ai.* Father Damien would then use this money to pay a *kokua* to pound the *pai ai* and mix the *poi* for the boys. He would also buy other food for the boys, such as flour, coffee and sugar. Hutchison recalled how they also baked bread: "The flour is made into bread and baked in a stone oven built of lava rocks by Father Damien a short distance away from the first dormitory and good yeast bread it was as any person can desire." As a result of their efforts, the boys "had a variety of food in quantity sufficient to eat their fill, *poi,* potatoes, bread, coffee, milk, beef, vegetables and fish salmon, no stint of food."

David Kamahana, who was sent to Kalaupapa in April, 1888, at the age of 13, recalled his first meeting with Father Damien, in which he was invited to go and eat with the boys.

> *I went to Kalawao and when Father Damien saw me he asked me if I had just arrived and where I was living. I answered "I live at Kalaupapa with my brother." Father Damien asked me: "Who is your brother?" I told him his name was Koalele. Father Damien said, "I know him. He is a good boy." So Father Damien told me to remain in Kalawao and to go and eat with the boys. I went in and I got my food with the boys, and so I saw Father Damien walking up and down to see if they had enough, otherwise he would call the helper to give them more . . .* [62]

Joseph Manu recalled: "He worked with boys without taking precautions and maybe he exposed himself to the infection. Anyway, it was not all imprudence since he did it wanting to be their father. He had no prudence as he had no fear of the disease while doing his work. He was linked to the patients as one of them."

Father Damien's presence also provided some consolation, someone for heartbroken parents to turn to for information and reassurance that their child was somehow all right.

If your kindness permits, good Father of the fatherless children of Kalawao, I am inquiring about the condition of a certain boy by the name of Kapoliola, who was taken from here to Kalawao, how he is getting along and whether he has some clothes or not. If you happen to see him, please give the aloha (love) of his grandparents and the family.[63] -- John, from Pauoa

Young girls at Kalaupapa. *Detail of photo, A. Law Collection*

I am asking you if my daughter Cecelia is at Kalawao or Kalaupapa? If you see her, I would like that you see she is taken good care of and also let us know of anything she needs.[64] -- Cecelia Haliimaile

I have told my two children to stay with you and hope that you will accept them. I am waiting for the Legislature and after that I expect to come to Molokai to be a helper to them.[65] -- S.H. Mookapu

I arrived here for the purpose of ascertaining whether my sons Paul Kahaulomoku and Ahunui are alive or dead. The rumor was that they are dead. A reply to the above will be greatly appreciated.[66] -- Victoria

I respectfully request your kindness to accept my son James Keohokalolo, former altar boy for Father Leonor at Kakaako. There are no signs of leprosy on him as you see him yourself. I trust that you will take good care of him.[67] -- D.K.M. Keohokalolo

Young boys at Kalaupapa. *Detail of photo, A. Law Collection*

It was a rather hard parting, when I left you and the family. I shall not forget the love and the good deeds you have done for the family. You are a real and true Father, a patient Father and a loving Father...[68] -- Mr. S. Hoopii

In 1881, Father Damien wrote to the father of 8 ½-year-old John Cullen: "I drop you these few lines to inform you that your boy, John is well and already used to our place . . ."[69] John Cullen lived to reach the age of 44, dying at Kalaupapa in 1917.

Father Damien was also sent other requests, such as that from Kuaana, a young girl who had been sent to the Kapiolani Home for Girls in Honolulu along with her sister, both of whom were deemed not to have leprosy. Another sister was still at Kalaupapa. Kuaana wrote: "Father, please tell our older sister there to make *lauhala* hats for us. She knows the measurements."[70]

The boys composed a Hawaiian song in honor of Father Damien which they sing on certain occasions. The boys had no string instruments like guitars, ukuleles or fiddles but the boys had tin pipe flutes, tenor and bass drums, steel triangle and bones with which they make music on, and named themselves the Kalawao Band.

Ambrose Hutchison

Chapter 8

Music and Celebration

Antone Pacheco. *Detail of photo, Hawai'i State Archives*

Amidst the poverty and loneliness of life at Kalaupapa, there was color, there was kindness, there was music and there was celebration. This was well illustrated in the Corpus Christi procession of 1874 that was organized by Father Damien and described by Father André Burgerman, who was at Kalaupapa in March of that year.

Two repositories draped with the colors of Hawaii had been prepared, one at the end of the peninsula, the other in the hospital enclosure. The canopy and portable altar were about nine feet high and made of bamboo which the men had found in the mountains. For lack of paint, they were decorated with red and white paper in spirals . . . At 3 o'clock, the procession started, divided into three groups. The first, with three banners and thirty oriflammes, was made up of the children, the young girls and adults. The second was that of the portable altar which followed the band and the men's and women's choirs. The third was the Blessed Sacrament. Four strong men, clad in green attire, ornamented with a large red cross, carried the canopy. At the four corners, acolytes in cassocks carried flags. In front, choir boys were swinging censers, preceded by little girls in blue and white who were throwing flowers. Another band closed the procession . . . The priest walked under the canopy . . . Tears covered his face . . .[71]

In 1875, when Bishop Maigret came for Confirmation, he was amazed at the reception that he received. Horsemen waited for him at the landing. A Mass of Mozart was sung in church. A procession with 200 people carrying flags conducted the Bishop to the boat, accompanied by the band.[72] In his diary, Bishop Maigret described a "moonlight serenade" after supper with 20 musicians and four bass drums.[73]

Music was always a part of life, and of death, at Kalawao. A visiting priest described the funeral of Juliana:

> *Gradually the procession approached; I could distinguish the big drums, the rattle of smaller ones, and wood and percussion instruments. Soon the church was full. Fr. Damien gave the absolution and the funeral started to the cemetery. Some women were holding the funeral pall. Others, in two rows, followed the body. All were dressed in black and wore either a red or white band according to which confraternity they belonged to. The band brought up the rear. The musicians seemed happy to play such excellent music for the good Christian they were burying. "Poor Juliana," Fr. Damien said to me afterwards, "she was so good…"*[74]

In 1881, Princess Liliuokalani visited Kalaupapa, where the people had "prepared a grand reception and turned out a body of cavalry 60 strong, dressed in red shirts and black pants . . . and a great crowd at the landing." The *Hawaiian Gazette* reported: "The Princess was very much overcome . . . and was quite unable to speak. The Hon. J.M. Kapena had to make an address on her behalf . . . Though much affected by what she saw, the Regent was very pleased to notice that these her unfortunate subjects were able to be so cheerful and happy . . ."[75] When Princess Liliuokalani returned to Honolulu, she had documents prepared in the name of her brother, King Kalakaua, that designated Father Damien a Knight Commander of the Royal Order of Kalakaua.[76] She also wrote to him personally to thank him for his efforts on behalf of her people:

> *I desire to express to you my admiration for the heroic and disinterested service you are rendering to the most unhappy of my subjects; and to pay, in some measure, a public tribute to the devotion, patience, and unbounded charity, with which you give yourself*

to the corporal and spiritual relief of these unfortunate people, who are necessarily deprived of the affectionate care of their relations and friends…[77]

Father Damien replied to Princess Liliuokalani that, although he felt unworthy, he would accept the honor because it was "a permanent and public testimony of the existing good understanding between the Royal family and the Catholic church."[78] Bishop Hermann Koeckemann traveled to Kalawao to present the medal to Father Damien, who went to upper Molokai to meet him. Father Damien described the crowd that welcomed them upon their return:

> *About noon, we began to descend this dangerous precipice by a narrow hollowed path, and on reaching the plain, were received by a body of horsemen, handsomely dressed and carrying banners… After an address of welcome, we moved on to Kalawao. There, at the entrance of the cemetery, where a triumphal arch had been erected, Father Albert Montiton awaited us with the women and children, who received his lordship with songs of welcome.*[79]

Ambrose Hutchison described how in the next year, 1882, the people of Kalaupapa initiated a new tradition. As plans were being made for the Corpus Christi celebration, which was traditionally attended only by Catholics, "the unexpected happened." A committee of those who were sick, "without distinction or creed started the collection of money" for a Hawaiian feast. Those who were able "willingly contributed their coin to a common fund and those who had no ready cash, promised to give in lieu of money, sweet potatoes, etc. for the feast . . ." The week before Corpus Christi Day, there was much activity among those who had leprosy and their helpers who were "willing to do their bit to make the celebration a success and memorable." The Church and stations were decorated with evergreens and ferns. The school house on the Mission ground was used for the feast and all food was prepared by the *mea kokua.* Food was delivered to everyone who was not able to attend. Ambrose Hutchison recalled:

> *At the forenoon 10 o'clock mass the Church was filled to overflowing for the first time since its enlargement… more people attended Church that Sunday than has been known*

in the past. The Hawaiian feast was no doubt the interesting cause of the Church being crowded with people. Mass over, the crowd was asked to go to the school house where food awaited them ... Poi, sweet potatoes, cooked pig, a la Hawaiian, cooked and uncooked pond mullets, shell fish (opihis), Kukui nut sauce ... When any one diner was out of any one article of food, more would be given ... Members of the Congregationalist Protestant Church of Kalaupapa after their prayer meeting came over to the Mission ground in a body and were received and feasted ...

After Mass at Kalawao, Father Damien and members of his congregation hastened to the Kalaupapa side of the peninsula where everybody was "welcome and feasted." Father Damien and Father Albert were given the head of a pig to feast on. Hutchison recalled:

Corpus Christi Celebration. *Damien Museum Archives*

After they had eaten of it, they declared it Par excellence. When the last bell rang for Vespers, the people sitting in groups about the mission ground arose to their feet to enter the Church. Catholics and Protestants mingled freely, all were Catholics for the moment, till every sitting space in the Church [was] filled ... in each succeeding year the celebration of the Corpus Christi was never without a luau, Hawaiian feast. It had come to stay as part of the festival ... alternately celebrated at Kalaupapa and at Kalawao with pomp.

Later that year, Father Damien described the Christmas celebration to his brother, Father Pamphile:

December 23: ... I find everybody waiting for me for Holy Mass, etc. After breakfast we have to clean up and decorate the church. Being short of artificial flowers, and other decorations, my young people bring me greenery from the woods which they make into long garlands. To cover the arch and part of the altar takes a half hour. The wooden candlesticks -- each with six candles -- are only waiting to be lighted at midnight Mass.

December 24: Sunday morning. Finishing touches on decorating the altar. I'm only half satisfied, since I have only old ornaments to put on it ... 11 o'clock at night the bell rings. Our young people go through the village beating two drums, waking everybody up and shouting "Merry Christmas!" The weather was beautiful. All my Catholics, all dressed up, hurry to church. At a quarter to twelve, the bell rings again. We begin our prayers together, soon my choir (at least twenty) begin their Christmas carols ... It is about 2 o'clock when all is over. Everybody went home happy and pleased. This is the tenth time we have had Midnight Mass here ...[80]

Ambrose Hutchison described the celebration of Hawaiian national holidays:

When a Hawaiian National Holiday is nigh ... the boys turn out with their instruments and station themselves in front of Father Damien's house. The playing of a lively tune on their tin flutes, steel, bones and drums break out on the silent morning air that aroused not only Father Damien but the whole neighborhood of the Kalawao Settlement from their peacefull slumber to hurriedly dress and rushed to the mission ground where the music racket is going on in full blast. Father Damien appears on the upper verandah of his house and his morning greeting to the boys below: "Poe keiki kolo-he [rascal children]." At the sound of his voice, the boys ceased playing on their instruments and the beautiful contralto voice of a youth by the name of Pake, the leading soloist of the Church choir, rings out clear like a soaring lark songster on the still morning air . . .

Father Damien is at attention during the singing of the song by his boys . . . Other Hawaiian songs follow after the singing of the first song, and the singing continues to the delight of the throng until the bell tolls, the songs treat ends. The assemblage enters the church for Mass. Mass over, the boys have their breakfast and the order of the day is for the boys to loaf about the home and amuse themselves in any way they desire. Some of the boys who have good feet and hands go fishing and return about noon or in the afternoon with their catches and shell fishes for all hands to feast on. On these holidays, Father Damien if he had anything on hand to give to his boys he would gladly do so, but very often it is the contrary, for he is as poor as his boys were.

Young men and boys in front of St. Philomena, "Father Damien's Church." *A. Law Collection*

Eia ae o Damiana ka makua o kakou

Here is Damien, Our Father

Composed by the Boys at Kalawao

Eia ae o Damiana,
Ka makua o kakou,
He poniponi na maka,
He alohilohi na aniani
Ke ike aku oe kau e ka lia.

A he ohana like kakou,
Na ka makua hookahi no,
Goodbye oe goodbye kakou,
A e huli hoi nei me ke aloha.

Ke hoonani ia ke Akua
Ka makua mana loa
Ma na lani kiekie, a e
Malu in a kanaka ma ka
Honua makemake i ka pono.

A he ohana like kakou,
Na ka makua hookahi no,
Goodbye oe goodbye kakou,
A e huli hoi nei me ke aloha

Here is Damien,
Our father,
His eyes are like the first glimmer of dawn,
Clear and sparkling
Upon seeing him, fond memories come to mind.

We are all like a family,
With one father,
Goodbye to you, goodbye to each of us,
May you return with aloha.

God be praised
The all-powerful parent
In the high heavens, and
Bringing peace to people
On earth who desire righteousness.

We are like a family,
With one father,
Good bye to you, goodbye to each of us,
May you return with aloha.

Recounted by Ambrose Hutchison in his memoirs
Translated from Hawaiian by Frances N. Frazier

Father Damien with young people, most likely in the hospital compound at Kalawao. *Photograph probably by H.L. Chase, c. 1878, Hawai`i State Archives*

The people here are supporting me in whatever I ask…
because of your good and charitable work for our people…

I pray to Almighty God to help us in this great work…
With best wishes to you and our beloved people. [81]

Queen Kapiolani to Father Damien, 1884

Chapter 9

Our Beloved People

Queen Kapiolani, *Detail of photo,*
Hawai'i State Archives

On July 19, 1884, Queen Kapiolani, Princess Liliuokalani and her husband Governor John Dominis, Dr. Eduard Arning and other officials arrived at Kalaupapa. According to Ambrose Hutchison: "The Queen was the first to step ashore from the boat followed by the others, greeted those present at the landing *'Aloha oukou'* (Love to all) and heartily returned in kind *'Aloha ke alii'* (Love to the chief)."

Hutchison, who had recently been appointed Resident Superintendent, welcomed Queen Kapiolani and her party and led the visitors to the Catholic Mission headquarters at Kalaupapa, which was located near the landing. He later recalled:

> *Father Damien who had arrived from Kalawao received the Queen and party at the gate of the mission ground and took them to the Mission House while the populace gathered on the ground shouting welcome (Alohas) to their Aliis (chiefs) where the distinguished visitors sat in chairs on the verandah facing the people to rest awhile. From the verandah of the Mission House Queen Kapiolani arose from her chair, moved to the front and stood above the verandah step, addressed her people present seated on the lawn of the mission ground.*

In her report to her brother, King Kalakaua, Princess Liliuokalani repeated the Queen's words:

With love I greet you all. My heart-felt sympathy and that of His Majesty the King, your Father, is with you in your affliction. The King has sent His Sister, the heir apparent, to accompany me in this mission, to show his love to you. I also bring to you the love of the people of Honolulu, the ladies and gentlemen, natives and foreigners, and those of the other islands who have assisted me in raising the necessary funds and contributions for your relief. I have been made familiar with your letters to me, and petitions to the Legislature, and whatever remarks you may have to make we will be pleased to hear them while we are with you. The principal object of this mission to your asylum is to know your condition, and to render such assistance as may be necessary for your comfort…

I am very glad and happy I came. We have work to do when we return to Honolulu. I ask your Alii (chief) to accompany me on my survey tour of your homes my dear people.[82]

Queen Kapiolani visited the home of each person, together with Ambrose Hutchison, who later recalled:

The Queen with the superintendent entered every house and hut at Kalaupapa and Makanalua inhabited by [the sick]. The Queen greeted the occupants, "Aloha," as she entered the house or hut and the Queen's greeting returned in kind, "aloha," with sobs. She would ask the state of their health and how they fared? The replies in general of the stricken people to the Queen's inquiry was "pilikia," the Hawaiian word that means hardship and suffering. The Queen seeing with her own eyes the poverty, squalor and squalid bare conditions of the homes of some of her people, was visibly affected, and her only comment heard of the scene she was witnessing was "Kaumaha nohoi!" (deep sorrow). She bore the strain courageously in her determination to see it through, [which] made a lasting impression on the mind of the lone eye-witness of the scene never to be forgotten.

While Ambrose Hutchison took Queen Kapiolani to visit each house, Father Damien looked after the rest of the visitors. The Queen and her party stayed the night in a new visitors' building and the next day, she visited every house in Kalawao, accompanied by Ambrose Hutchison. She also visited the hospital which was, according to Hutchison, "bare of such needed necessities as beds and beddings…" He described the Queen's reaction to this hospital, that was supposed to help her people in the last stages of their illness.

> *The Queen approached the patients with solemn Aloha and received response with sobs*
> *from some of the patients and others regarded their Queen silently. Mutually drawn*
> *by instinctive sympathy, the Queen went through the entire Hospital buildings, peeks in*
> *the dying den and told the name of the shack, she shuddered and expressed her horror*
> *in no uncertain terms…*

Taken in 1884, this photo is probably of the visit of Queen Kapiolani and her party. Historian Colette Higgins has speculated that Queen Kapiolani is the woman on the horse at the far right. Siloama, the Protestant Church, is pictured with St. Philomena Church in the background. *Detail of photo, A. Law Collection*

In her Report to the King, Princess Liliuokalani listed nine recommendations. These included increasing the food and clothing allowances, improving the water supply, providing a resident physician and assistant, obtaining Sisters of Mercy, enlarging the hospital, providing an ambulance to transport those who had disabilities, and providing other wagons to deliver food.

Queen Kapiolani was deeply moved by her visit to Kalaupapa. Upon her return to Honolulu, she apparently asked Father Damien to compile a list of the people at the Settlement who needed help. Father Damien wrote in "flawless" Hawaiian to Queen Kapiolani, "the Royal Mother of the People Suffering," on August 6, 1884:

> *Your letter is in the hands of your obedient servant. I have fulfilled your requests. That is, I have finished the catalogue of names of the sick people imploring the mercy of their mother. Through the offices of the Board of Health, you will receive a list of all the people who are sick living here, with the annotation of the date and place of their birth…*[83]

Five days later, the Queen wrote to Father Damien:

> *The people here are supporting me in whatever I ask for… because of your good and charitable work for our people. Give my best regards to our friends there when you meet them. Who are the patients of the hospital that died recently? Do you want some furniture for the house and plants?*[84]

By October, the Queen wrote that they had made clothing for those who were identified as in need.

> *In your last letter you mentioned the fact that there are 187 men and 93 women who are entitled to the allotments of clothes… Each man will receive a shirt, a pair of trousers and a blanket and each woman a dress, a slip and a blanket. As to the needs of the helpers (kokuas), we shall consider them later… May Almighty God help us in this great work. With best wishes to you and our people…*[85]

Also recommended in Princess Liliuokalani's report was the establishment of a home for children born at the Settlement who showed no signs of the disease. The Kapiolani Home for Girls was formally opened on the grounds of the Kakaako Branch Hospital in Honolulu on November 9, 1885, with ten girls from Kalaupapa.

The keys of the Home were presented on a crimson velvet cushion to Queen Kapiolani. She unlocked the door and presented the keys to Mother Marianne Cope, who had come to Hawaii from New York in1883. King Kalakaua then decorated Mother Marianne with the Order of Kapiolani, an Order established by the King to reward acts of benevolence on behalf of his people.[86] In the two short years she had been in Hawaii, Mother Marianne and her fellow Sisters of St. Francis had transformed the Kakaako Branch Hospital into a modern, sanitary facility where people were cared for, comforted, and supported emotionally.

ORIGINAL CRIMSON VELVET PILLOW ON WHICH RESTED THE KEYS TO KAPIOLANI HOME FOR FEMALE CHILDREN OF LEPROSY PATIENTS, KAKAAKO, HONOLULU.
Presented to Mother Marianne by Her Majesty Queen Kapiolani on the Home's opening day, November 9, 1885.

The crimson pillow on which rested the keys to the Kapiolani Home that were presented to Mother Marianne by Queen Kapiolani. The pillow is on display at the Blessed Marianne Cope Museum in Syracuse, New York. *Photo by Henry Law*

Father Damien . . . stepped ashore from the boat. He had his left foot bandaged. Mutual greeting passed between us. Naturally I asked the Father how he hurt his foot? And came the prompt answer, I did it with hot water. Hot water, said I, surprised. Yes, while at the Mission. I had taken a tub and poured some hot water in it to wash my feet. I put my foot into the water. I did not feel the heat and I did not know it was too hot. The result is as you see. I blistered my foot and he added, calling me by name with a touch of irony, "I think I have the disease," and limped away . . .

Ambrose Hutchison

Chapter 10

We Will Take Care of Him

Mother Marianne Cope, c. 1885.
Detail of photo, A. Law Collection

Mother Marianne Cope arrived in Honolulu on November 8, 1883. She was 45 years old, two years older than Father Damien, and already a proven leader, innovator and pioneer of social justice. A woman of great vision, she had helped to start two of the first 50 hospitals in the United States -- St. Elizabeth's in Utica, New York, and St. Joseph's in Syracuse. She had also been elected Provincial Superior of her Order, the Sisters of St. Francis of Syracuse, in 1877 and re-elected unanimously in 1881.

Mother Marianne chose six Sisters to accompany her to Hawaii: Sister M. Crescentia Eilers, Sister M. Bonaventure Caraher, Sister M. Renata Nash, Sister M. Rosalia McLaughlin, Sister M. Ludovica Gibbons, and Sister M. Antonella Murphy. This small band of Sisters would become the first members of a religious community founded in the United States to initiate mission work in a foreign land.

Just a few months after the Sisters' arrival, the *Pacific Commercial Advertiser* described the reluctance of many to leave Kakaako, as demonstrated in a meeting held with Queen Kapiolani and Walter Murray Gibson, President of the Board of Health. Reverend Kauwa spoke to the Queen on behalf of himself and others at Kakaako:

He said that since the good and religious women had come (the Sisters of Charity) who were constant in their care and attention of them, their hearts had revived and many were now hopeful of health who had formerly despaired and therefore there was such a sad and painful feeling to leave this well ordered hospital and these kind and gentle Sisters who waited on them like Angels. He then lifted up his hands and read a short and impressive prayer.[87]

Gathered together in front of the Kapiolani Home, located on grounds of Kakaako Hospital, are (back row, left to right): Sr. M. Martha Kaiser, Sister M. Leopoldina Burns, Sr. M. Rosalia McLaughlin, Sr. M. Crescentia Eilers, Mother Marianne Cope, and Sr. M. Charles Hoffmann. Pictured with them is Walter Murray Gibson, who was instrumental in bringing the Sisters to Hawaii. Pictured in the front row are the first ten girls sent to the Kapiolani Home from Kalaupapa, including the youngest, Ana Iopa (far right). *Hawai`i State Archives*

Residents of the Kakaako Branch Hospital. *Photograph by Dr. Eduard Arning, Damien Museum Archives and Museum für Völkerkunde Hamburg*

King Kalakaua and Queen Kapiolani were frequent visitors to the Kakaako Branch Hospital and worked closely with Mother Marianne. The *Pacific Commercial Advertiser* described a visit by the King and Queen in 1885.

> *They arrived shortly before 11 o'clock, and as their carriage passed through the gate house the inmates of the hospital that were able to be out cheered their visitors very heartily… After a chat with the good Mother and Sisters their Majesties visited all the sick wards accompanied by the Mother Superior and Mr. Gibson…*
>
> *The attention of the royal visitors was attracted by the tasteful manner in which the grounds have been laid out. On either side of the entrance to the chapel are flower beds shaped as anchor, cross, and heart; emblems of Truth, Hope and Charity, while on the grass plot oppose are also cut flower beds forming in large letters the inscription Aloha. Seeing these and also the names Kalakaua and Kapiolani thus cut out in the sward*

The grounds of the Kakaako Hospital, showing the new double swing set in the center.   *Hawaiʻi State Archives*

[lawn], the Queen remarked that there might also be cut a motto to commemorate their visit, and His Majesty wrote down the words HOOLA LAHUI (HEAL THE NATION), which were handed to the Mother Superior, and they will form a new inscription in the grounds. While passing through the refectory and in the kitchen their Majesties examined critically the arrangements made for preparing and serving the food…

They were particularly pleased with the cleanliness and order seen in this department. There has been lately set up in the kitchen a large and well designed range for cooking, which is a great improvement over the old style kettles used heretofore. These kettles are utilized by the Sisters in making soap, a large quantity of which is manufactured from the fat obtained in cooking.

Passing by a double swing that has lately been put up at the end of the main avenue, the royal visitors looked into the bright, clean school room built for the children at

Kakaako, and then paused for a few minutes to exchange greetings with the female patients gathered on the verandas of the neat cottages in which they live. The Queen recognized among them an old acquaintance, and towards her, as well as the rest of the poor victims of this dread, mysterious malady, her kindly sympathetic nature was shown in her questions regarding their condition and the thanks that she, as well as His Majesty, tendered to the Mother Superior and her Sisters for what they had done and were doing... As the King and Queen passed in front of each group of cottages they were received by the patients with alohas and other characteristic Hawaiian salutations.[88]

Schoolgirls at Kakaako Branch Hospital, June, 1885. *Photo by Dr. Eduard Arning, Hawaiian Historical Society and Museum für Völkerkunde Hamburg*

Research into leprosy was conducted and new treatments were also being tried at Kakaako. On a visit to Japan in 1881, King Kalakaua had learned of the Goto bath treatments and towards the end of 1885, Dr. Masanao Goto arrived in Hawaii to introduce his medicated baths at Kakaako.[89] Earlier that year, Father Damien had been officially diagnosed with leprosy. He wrote to Bishop Koeckemann: "As I have no doubt of the real character of the malady, I remain calm, resigned, and very happy in the midst of my people. The good God knows what is best for my sanctification, and I say daily, *Fiat voluntas tua* [Thy will be done], with a ready heart."[90]

Dr. Arthur Mouritz commented on the circumstances that he felt resulted in Father Damien contracting the disease and, at the same time, provided strong testimony to counteract rumors by some that Father Damien's leprosy was due to immoral behavior.

> *Father Damien was often sick through dysentery and diarrhea, yet struggled on and wouldn't give up. There was no one else to do the work -- no nurses, no doctors. Without doubt this continuous exposure made him more susceptible to leprosy. Father Damien was obstinate and wouldn't give up …*
>
> *I used to warn him to be more careful … He did not heed my warnings because he had his own ideas about the danger of contagion and his duties as a priest … If Father Damien had escaped leprosy it would have been miraculous …*

NUMBER	NAME	SEX		NATIONALITY		AGE IN	ADMITTED		
		Male	Female	Hawaiian	Foreigner	Years	MONTH	DAY	A. D.
TOTAL									
02881	Kaaiape	K		yes		50	Mar.	30	1886
02882	Kahakai	K		yes		60	"	"	"
02883	Kunui	K		yes		57	"	"	"
02884	Nakilau	K		yes		50	"	"	"
02885	Kapahu	K		yes		40	"	"	"
02886	Father Damien	K			Belgian	45	"	"	"
02887	Manaia	K		yes		20	"	"	"
02888	Keakaulaiwi	K		yes		38	Apr	23	"
02889	Kamakaanapu	K		yes		26			

The register where Father Damien was officially "admitted" to Kalaupapa as Number 2886 on March 30, 1886, more than a year after he was officially diagnosed with leprosy. *Hawai'i State Archives*

Regardless of the danger of contagion, Father Damien lived and labored alongside a cemetery of a thousand bodies… With only a foot of earth to cover them… he received visitors who took food from his table and smoked his pipe…

He allowed men and women and boys and girls to sit around his house and come into his house as if a hotel. Father Damien saw no danger in this and did it because of his love… and his kindheartedness. In fact, there were so many people around his house that it would have been impossible to have done anything wrong, this was true in the night time as well as the day time. I myself called [at] his house all the time… I had free access to Father Damien's rooms at all hours both day and night, on the priest's premises there were no locked doors nor screened windows. During the night the lights in his house were always on, the boys dormitories were right up against Father Damien's house, the windows and doors of his house were open night and day. [91]

In early 1886, Father Damien expressed the desire to go to Kakaako to be confessed and try the Goto baths. His religious superior, Father Leonor Fouesnel informed him that it had been decided by the Provincial Council that if he came to Honolulu, he would either have to be confined at Kakaako or in a room at the Catholic Mission. In addition, he noted that neither he nor Father Clement Evrard would "consent to say Mass with the same chalice and the same vestments you have used." Father Leonor continued: "Your intentions prove to us that you possess neither delicacy nor charity towards your neighbor and that you think only of yourself."[92]

Father Leonor's letter hurt Father Damien deeply. He wrote to Bishop Hermann Koeckemann:

The absolute refusal expressed in the tones of a policeman rather than of an Honorable religious Superior, and that in the name of the Bishop and of the minister as if the mission were going to be put in quarantine if ever I showed myself in Honolulu -- gave me, I confess it frankly, more pain than all I have had to suffer since my childhood… I still await Our Lord, through the intercession of our good Mother, to perform a miracle in my favor, but alas, I am not worthy. [93]

Dr. Mouritz was well aware of Father Damien's anguish and wrote to Bishop Koeckemann in hopes of arousing his sympathy.

> *I take the liberty of suggesting to you that in my opinion it would be good to send Father Damien to Kakaako, especially to take the baths there everyday and to put him in another milieu . . . Things seem very critical for him and there is little hope. The leprosy progresses rapidly and I am sure that you will be alarmed in noticing the rapid change of his whole exterior. His life is so monotonous and hard here, that a little relaxation and the little attentions of the Sisters will do him much good, in my opinion.*[94]

In early July, Father Damien expressed his determination to go Kakaako to Rudoph Meyer, who supervised the management of the Settlement from his home on upper Molokai. Meyer advised him to travel from Kaunakakai to Honolulu on the *Mokolii* since it was less probable that anyone would say anything about it. Meyer added: "I am going to Kaunakakai on Saturday and if you come early, I shall be glad of your company . . ."[95]

On July 11, Walter Murray Gibson wrote in his diary: "Father Damien arrived at Kakaako . . . was advised not to come -- but was determined to visit the Sisters. I begin to doubt the genuineness of his religious devotion."[96] When Gibson expressed his displeasure to Mother Marianne over Father Damien's proposed visit, she simply replied: "Send him here. We will take care of him. Do not do anything that can hurt his feelings. He has suffered more than anyone can imagine."[97]

During the five days that he was at Kakaako, Father Damien spent many long hours talking with Mother Marianne. At a time when others seemed intent on rejecting him and treating him as if he was different now that he had leprosy, as if he had somehow become inferior, Mother Marianne spent hours listening to him. She clearly understood Father Damien's sense of urgency as he talked about the future, about his concerns, about his people at Kalawao, about the children and what would happen to them when he was gone, and about his fervent hope that the Sisters would finally be allowed to go to Kalaupapa.

Mother Marianne Cope on the porch of the Kapiolani Home for Girls, c. 1885. *Detail of photo, A. Law Collection*

When Father Damien returned to Kalawao, he felt renewed and enthusiastic. The Goto baths had made him feel better and he was anxious to establish them at Kalawao. Kakaako had been good for him physically, but even better for him emotionally. He now had hope -- hope in a new treatment but, even more important, hope that Mother Marianne and the other Sisters would soon come to Kalaupapa.

The decision regarding whether or not the Sisters should go to Kalaupapa was caught up in politics and the preconceived ideas of many men in power who felt that it was simply not appropriate to send women to the Settlement unless, of course, they had leprosy. Mother Marianne had always been willing to go to Kalaupapa. From the beginning, she had specified that this was her intent. She was not afraid. The Sisters did not need the protection of men. God had led them; He would protect them. Mother Marianne knew that she and the Sisters could deal with the hardships as well, if not better, than many men of their time, but it would take two more years before the Sisters would finally be given permission to go to Kalaupapa. In the meantime, as she saw people continue to be taken from Kakaako to Kalaupapa, Mother Marianne often sent a note along with a child or young person asking that they be taken to Father Damien upon arrival. Dr. Mouritz recounted the story of little girl named Mary.

> *I was at the landing, waiting in the lee of the freight house, sheltered from wind and rain, when I was accosted by a diminutive, girlish figure, asking if I was Father Damien, as she carried a letter from the Sisters at Kakaako detention station for him. This little girl, not full ten years old, told a pitiful story -- she was soaked to the skin with rain and sea, and shivering with cold, was anxious to get food, shelter and a place to sleep. She was self-possessed, informed me her father had died on the steamer, and was buried at Pukoo, a port of the lee side of Molokai; also on the steamer, too ill to be landed was her little brother 6 years old...*

> *I speedily passed her along to Father Damien and some kokua women who fed and warmed the child and gave her dry clothing. Her brother was landed at daylight much to the child's delight. The little girl's name was Mary, and her great dread and worry was that she would have no house to shelter her, hence the letter to Father Damien from the Sisters asking him to exercise his good offices in getting this family settled.[95]*

Two children at Kalaupapa in later years. *A. Law Collection*

Holy oils -- Baptismal water -- Cloth -- Towels -- tools -- Crackers -- fruit -- Leather -- Rope -- strings -- wire -- nails -- screws -- nuts -- washers -- pens, Ink -- most anything you might call for -- no matter what size -- could be fished out of that bag.[99]

Joseph Dutton, describing the old and worn haversack canvas bag with a shoulder strap that Father Damien always carried

Chapter 11

The Sicker He Got,
The Harder He Worked

Father Damien in February, 1889.
Photo by William T. Brigham, Damien Museum Archives

Father Damien knew his time was limited and according to Dr. Mouritz: "... the sicker he got the harder he worked. If he had rested more when sick, he would have lasted longer. He wore himself out working, overtaxing his human strength to do God's work."[100]

Over the years, three priests worked at the Settlement with Father Damien for varying periods of time -- Father André Burgerman, Father Albert Montiton, and Father Gregory Archambaux. Coming shortly after Father Damien's leprosy was officially confirmed, Father Albert's departure in March, 1885, left Father Damien without assistance, just at the time that he needed it the most.

On July 29, 1886, about two weeks after Father Damien returned from Kakaako, a 43-year-old Civil War veteran, dressed in a simple blue denim suit, arrived at Kalaupapa. For the next 44 years, Joseph Dutton did not leave the peninsula, seeking to do penance for what he referred to as a "degenerate decade" in his life.[101] Dr. Mouritz described his first impressions of Dutton: "The day of his arrival, Br. Dutton took luncheon with me, and I scanned him carefully. He had come afoot from Kaunakakai [upper Molokai] . . . he was reserved and thoughtful, had nothing to say about his past life nor the reason for his seeking seclusion and work at Molokai, and turning his back on the world forever."[102]

According to Ambrose Hutchison, Joseph Dutton and Father Damien met for the first time the next day and Dutton lived in the visitors' quarters for three months while Father Damien built his cottage. Hutchison described Dutton's initial work at Kalawao. A lean to shed stood between Father Damien's house and his church where people would sit on benches arranged on three sides with their feet and hands in tubs filled with warm, medicated water. Hutchison observed how Dutton watched Father Damien gently tend to the people, bathing and sponging their sores with the warm medicated water. After being allowed to dry, a salve was spread, and clean cotton bandages were applied. Hutchison observed: "After standing aloof for some days, the urge to follow the example of Father Damien was irresistible. Mr. Dutton went to work with a will and in a couple of weeks time became an adept washer and dresser of sores that relieved Father Damien of the work . . ."

What appears to be the lean-to-shed can be seen between Father Damien's two-story house and the church. Father Damien is in the foreground. *Detail of photo by Dr. Eduard Arning, c. 1884, Hawaiian Historical Society and Museum für Völkerkunde Hamburg*

Father Damien was clearly appreciative of Dutton's help and friendship. In a letter to Father Daniel Hudson at the University of Notre Dame, Father Damien commented: "The courage of my Dear brother Joseph Ira B. Dutton appears to respond very well to the special calling for which our Blessed Lord has chosen him. He takes a special interest in all what concerns the altars and sacristies of our churches . . . and He's truly a good confrere to me."[103]

Joseph Dutton, in later years, on the grounds of the Baldwin Home for men and boys at Kalawao. *Detail of photo, Hawai'i State Archives*

One of their initial projects was to establish the Goto baths at Kalawao. Dutton later recalled:

> *Tubs of redwood were made with little stones set into the sides . . . A partly inclosed little house was fixed up close by the back door of Father Damien's two story residence. The men and women coming to bathe at certain hours and waiting for each other to go in the partly inclosed little house or shelter. Some months later we got a better bath house ready -- in compartments -- close by the church. Then Father Damien began to take the baths himself in one of these compartments. Things in general were very crude in those days . . .*[104]

Father Damien described the Goto baths as a "ray of hope" and, two months after returning from Kakaako, noted that about 60 people were enjoying these warm baths, morning and evening, for about 15 minutes each. He asked for one ton of coal and added: "The majority under treatment are doing very well and the change is very perceptible." He referred to Dutton as their "Japanese druggist" and asked for more Japanese medicine. He also added that if the Board of Health could not provide for the costs of building facilities for the Goto baths, "please let me know and Christian charity will be called in."[105]

One of Father Damien's benefactors was Reverend H.B. Chapman in England, who provided him with funds at different times. In December, 1888, Father Damien thanked Rev. Chapman for the £975 recently received which he planned to use to buy warm clothing for his people: "I greatly thank the charitable donors . . . by the arrival of those goods the scent of the flower of English love will be greatly appreciated and long remembered by a great many . . . whose cold and benumbed limbs will feel again the comfort of warm cloth . . ."[106] About four months later, Dutton informed Father Hudson: "Quite an amount of money has been received from England -- $4,727.27 in bank at Honolulu."[107]

While he had a remarkable ability to raise money when needed from outside sources, Father Damien lived and worked very simply. David Ilihia remembered: "He worked as a carpenter. Instead of wasting money for the job, he did it himself. I saw him build the church. Prepare the cement, saw wood -- he himself worked as an ordinary worker. Instead of using the horse to visit people, he walked most of the time."

Pohaku Melemai remembered: "His clothes were always mended and repaired and thus he practiced poverty. He used to conserve everything with care and not waste anything. I saw this myself . . ."

Although Father Damien was criticized by his superiors for exaggerating the situation at Kalawao, making it seem worse than it was, Father Damien knew the reality and persevered. In February, 1887, desperate, running out of time, and completely worn out by the bureaucracy that would not allow the Sisters to come to the Settlement, Father Damien let it be known that there were thoughts of having Anglican Sisters from England come to Kalaupapa.

The shell that was used as a holy water font by Father Damien. According to Joseph Dutton, it was fastened to a post near the front door of the first wooden addition to St. Philomena Church built by Father Damien, underneath the steeple, and was used by everyone. *Wisconsin Historical Society*

Bishop Koeckemann wrote to the Superior General about Father Damien's "impatience" but noted how he himself had maintained "a great reserve . . . almost passive" about sending the Franciscan Sisters, although Mother Marianne was very willing to have three Sisters go to Molokai. He also stated that Father Damien had "spoken very much even with exaggeration of the material misery" of the people at the Settlement.[108]

Father Leonor complained about Father Damien to the Superior General: "This good Father makes himself pass as consoler, providence, the nurse, the undertaker, the grave digger and he is nothing of the kind. He deserves high praise for the sacrifice he has made of his existence, his liberty, his life, but unfortunately those praises have reached him; he has gobbled them up, and become drunk with them, and now he is becoming dangerous."[109] Father Leonor warned Father Damien: ". . . you ought as far as you can [to] cease your correspondence with the exterior world. This affair can become more disastrous than you suppose."[110]

Determined to have others in place at the Settlement before he died, Father Damien had been corresponding with Father Lambert Conrardy for many years. In 1888, he finally wrote to the Bishop and insisted that Father Conrardy come to the Settlement immediately: "I need him right away . . . I humbly beg you to let him come as soon as he can . . . The circumstances I am in are exceptional; why can he not come to my aid through ways that are a little exceptional?"[111] Father Conrardy arrived on May 17, 1888.

Dr. Mouritz described the depression Father Damien experienced, in large part due to disappointment, frustration, a sense of urgency about the time he had left, and a real "grief" over the fact that the Sisters had not yet arrived.

> *He experienced earthly depression but this did not shake his faith and hope in God. Father Damien at times had the delusion, that is, the false impression that he was unworthy of heaven. Little things troubled him and he shed tears, but there was no question of real dejection; he was grieved because the Sisters failed to arrive when he expected them in July, 1886 -- they came Nov. 14, 1888, five months before Father Damien's death; he was also grieved because the Brothers did not come and because Dr. Goto's treatment had failed to cure him and the other[s] . . . also the petty difficulties with Joseph Dutton and the Board of Health who impeded improvements. He was also grieved at his helplessness and approaching death because he saw he could not accomplish all he wanted to . . .*[112]

While Dr. Mouritz noted Father Damien's depression, he also described the great fortitude with which he continued his work. This was illustrated in December, 1887, when Father Damien asked for 1,000 bricks so that he could build a bakery that would supply the people with good bread. In August, 1888, Father Damien wrote to Father Daniel Hudson at Notre Dame University about their work to again expand the church at Kalawao. He wrote that a "good old Irish man," probably Jack Lewis McMillan, was the mason, while "I with two of my boys do the wood work. If Allmigh[ty] God prolongs our days -- and maintains our strength. We hope to leave a good spacious church for those who may come after us . . ."[113]

Kenso Seki (left) and Hyman Fujinaga, both of whom were sent to Kalaupapa as young boys, participate in ceremonies to mark the 100th anniversary of Father Damien's death and the restoration of his church. Also pictured is Sister Davilyn Ah Chick, O.S.F. *Photo by A. Law*

Father Damien's Church more than 110 years after his death. *Photo by Henry Law*

With a donation from Charles Reed Bishop, the Bishop Home for girls was finished in September, 1888. This home was sometimes referred to as the "Pauahi Home" by the residents of Kalaupapa, most likely reflecting the fact that the donation for the Bishop Home had come from the estate of Bishop's wife, the late Princess Bernice Pauahi Bishop.[114]

Mother Marianne together with Sisters Vincent and Leopoldina finally prepared to leave the Kakaako Branch Hospital. On November 13, 1888, they boarded the *Lehua* together with Father Matthias Limburg and 47 individuals who had leprosy, 23 of whom were girls under the age of 16, including 5-year-old Kina Kamaka. Also on board were two 90-year-old men who would die within months of their arrival.[115]

When they arrived at Kalaupapa the next morning, they were met by Father Damien, who had come from Kalawao, and many of the women and children they had known at Kakaako. Father Matthias described Father Damien's spirits that day: "He had just recovered from a fever a few days previous, had not been at Kalaupapa for six weeks on account of his sickness. He seemed to revive and forget all suffering and illness for joy at the arrival of the sisters."[116]

Residents of the Bishop Home. *Detail of photo, A. Law Collection*

The Bishop Home provided comfort and a place of respite for hundreds of women and girls. This photograph was taken in 1904. *A. Law Collection*

He had great hope in God as he always prayed God to obtain what he wanted, as well as in his sufferings. This is the reason why he always was so strong and courageous in his work. He never lost courage. I know because I saw him. Great must have been his love for others, as he never ceased to comfort, encourage and visit them in their houses and he was prepared to sacrifice all to alleviate their sufferings. When they were near to death, he prayed with them and for them.

David Ilihia, a member of the Mormon Church, who was sent to Kalawao at the age of 23, just months before Father Damien died

Father Damien and Mother Marianne.
Damien Museum Archives

Chapter 12

A Final Christmas

Christmas, 1888, reflected the development of a deep sense of community at Kalaupapa and Kalawao. Members of different religions worked together and those who had leprosy worked in partnership with those who did not. Dr. Emerson, President of the Board of Health sent a letter to a Committee whom he asked to distribute gifts. The chairman was Ambrose Hutchison, Resident Superintendent. The other members of the Committee were Postmaster William Clark, who had been sent to Kalaupapa in 1886; Mother Marianne; Rev. J. Hanaloa, the Protestant minister; and "Rev. Father Damien or his substitute."[117]

The Board of Health and other friends in Honolulu, send their Christmas greetings to you, and through you to all the afflicted...

The "Lehua" or some other steamer will convey to you a quantity of gifts for the children, boys and girls at the Settlement, as an expression of their sympathy and aloha, and as a proof that they desire you not to be left out in the cold in the celebration of this glad anniversary. I would request you, whose names are placed at the head of this sheet, to act as a committee to see that the various things are fairly and wisely distributed among the children. A Merry Christmas to you all...

People did their best to make Christmas happy, but gifts could not replace parents or children. William Clark, who had been chosen to help distribute the gifts, must have been thinking of his own four children whom he was forced to leave behind two years earlier when he was sent to Kalaupapa.

William Clark pictured with his four children before he was sent to Kalaupapa. *Courtesy Kelli Wicke Davis*

Another father, Francisco Camacho sent a tin of crackers and some toys to Father Damien for his son's first Christmas at Kalaupapa: "Dear Father Damien, I am very grateful to you for the care of my child in the strange land without any hope for our seeing him again in this world. So Father good-bye for the present and tell Peter that we all send our love and greetings to him from his brother and sisters. Tell him that they did never forget him for a moment from the day he left Honolulu till this moment."[118]

Father Damien and the boys of Kalawao in February, 1889. *Photo by William T. Brigham, Bishop Museum Archives*

For two weeks over Christmas, the English artist Edward Clifford visited Kalawao, having read about Father Damien in a magazine of the Soho Girls Club. Clifford described his experience at Kalawao in a book he published the next year.[119]

> *"There is Father Damien!" said our purser; and slowly moving along the hillside, I saw a dark figure with a large straw hat. He came rather painfully down, and sat near the water-side, and we exchanged friendly signals across the waves, while my baggage was being got out of the hold -- a long business, for owing to the violence of the sea, nothing else was to be put on shore ... At last all was ready, and we went swinging across the waves, and finally chose a fit moment for leaping on shore. Father Damien caught me by the hand and a hearty welcome shone from his kindly face as he helped me up the rock. He immediately called me by my name "Edward," and said it was like everything else, "a providence," that he had met me at that irregular landing-place, for he had expected the ship to stop at Kalaupapa, and Father Conrardy had gone there ...*

His own little four-roomed house almost joins the church, and here Father Conrardy, who lives on the ground-floor, and who is a man of considerable refinement, met us, and ushered us into the tiny refectory where a meal was prepared. Here we found Brother James, a tall powerful-looking Irishman, who pleased me greatly by his simple earnestness, and by the intense affection which he bore to Father Damien.

By Father Damien's desire we sat at a separate table, as a precaution against infection; but he was close by, and we were all very happy together . . . After dinner we went up the little flight of steps which led to Father Damien's balcony. This was shaded by a honeysuckle in blossom. A door from it led into the sitting-room -- a busy-looking place, with a big map of the world -- and inside it another door opened on his bedroom.

Some of my happiest times at Molokai were spent in this little balcony, sketching him and listening to what he said . . . While I sketched him he often read his breviary. At other times we talked on subjects that interested us both, especially the work of the Church Army, and sometimes I sang hymns to him . . . I need scarcely say that he gives himself no airs of martyr, saint or hero -- a humbler man I never saw . . . He seldom talked of himself except in answer to questions and he had always about him the simplicity of a great man -- "clothed with humility."

. . . In the day-time at Molokai, one sees the people sitting chatting at their cottage doors, pounding the taro root, to make it into their favorite food poi, or galloping on their little ponies -- men and women alike astride -- between the two villages. And one always receives the ready greeting and the readier smile . . .

There are several churches, and the faces one sees are nearly always happy faces . . . There is a large general shop where tinned fruits and all sorts of things can be bought. The food no doubt, is somewhat monotonous in quality, and it pleases me to remember how Father Damien enjoyed some raisins I had brought from America . . .

Shortly after Christmas, Father Damien visited the Bishop Home for the last time. He commented on the girls in their pretty blue dresses with red ribbons and how they had

Riders on the road that leads from Kalaupapa to Kalawao. *Detail of photo, Hawai'i State Archives*

never had anything so nice in the Settlement prior to the Sisters' arrival. He had finished his church and was at peace. On February 19, 1889, he wrote his last letter to his brother, Father Pamphile: "I am quite happy and contented, and though seriously ill, all I desire is the accomplishment of the holy will of God . . . I am still able, but not without some difficulty, to stand every day at the altar, where I do not forget any of you . . . May God strengthen me, and give me the grace of perseverance and of a happy death."[120]

In addition to the Sisters, Father Wendelin Moellers had arrived at Kalaupapa on November 20 to serve as their chaplain and priest for the Kalaupapa parish. By this time, James Sinnett, who Father Damien also called "Brother," had also volunteered to work at the Settlement. But it was the presence of Mother Marianne and the Sisters that enabled Father Damien to finally let go.

Father Wendelin described Father Damien's last days:

"How good God is!" He said to me in the course of the day; "to have preserved me long enough to have two priests by my side to assist me in my last moments, and then to know that the good Sisters of Charity are at the hospital -- that was my Nunc dimittis [permission to depart] The work… is assured, I am no longer necessary…" I begged him to leave me his mantle, like Elias, that I might inherit his great heart. "But what would you do with it?" he asked; "it is full of leprosy." Then I asked him for his blessing, which he gave me with tears in his eyes. He also blessed the heroic daughters of St. Francis, for whose coming he had so long prayed.

The following day the good Father rallied a little; we even had hopes of keeping him for a time amongst us. The good Sisters often visited him. What I most admired in him was his admirable patience…

A rosary that hung in Father Damien's house. *Wisconsin Historical Society*

On Saturday, April 13, he was much worse, and all hope of improvement was at an end. Shortly after midnight he received our Lord in Holy Communion for the last time. Soon he was to see Him face to face. From time to time he lost consciousness. When I went to see him he recognized me, and spoke to me, and we took leave of one another, as I had to go to Kalaupapa for the following day, which was Sunday. On the morrow, after the services were over, I returned and found the good Father fairly strong, but his mind was somewhat confused. I could see in his eyes resignation, joy, and contentment, but his lips could no longer articulate the acts which his heart was making. Now and then he would affectionately press my hand.

On Monday, April 15, I received a note from Father Conrardy, saying that the good Father was in his agony. I hurried off to see him, but on my way another messenger met me, and informed me of his death. He died without a struggle, as if falling asleep . . .[121]

Father Damien was clothed in his cassock and at about 11:00 his body was taken to the church. Joseph Manu recalled: "When he died I was in Pelekunu, and when the news arrived, I came immediately to Kalawao, where I saw his body solemnly exposed on a table while they prepared the coffin. I looked to his face, when alive covered by leprosy, now completely clean and free of any trace of leprosy. First I couldn't believe my eyes and I looked again and finally I convinced myself."

Father Wendelin concurred: "When I arrived he was already dressed in his soutane [cassock]. All signs of leprosy had disappeared from his face . . . "[122] In the afternoon, Mother Marianne and the Sisters arrived and set to work, caring for Father Damien one last time. In her Journal, Sister Leopldina described how Mother Marianne transformed a rough wooden box into a beautiful casket, lined with white satin and edged with white lace.[123]

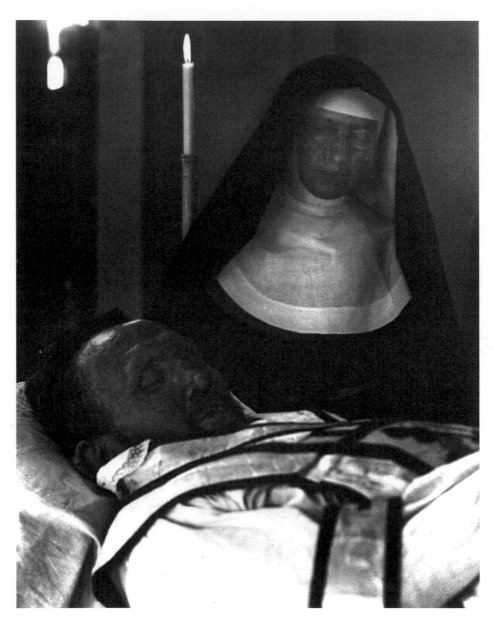

Father Damien lying in state at St. Philomena Church, supported by Mother Marianne.
Photo by Dr. S.B. Swift, Damien Museum Archives

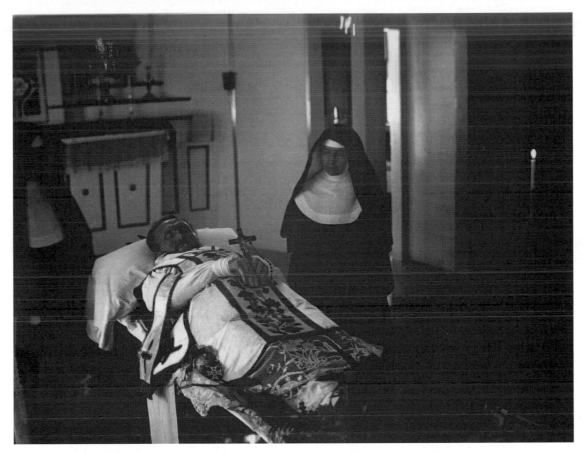

Mother Marianne (right) and Sister Leopoldina with Father Damien. *Photo by Dr. S.B. Swift, Damien Museum Archives*

When they returned home, despite the fact that she had been on her feet all day, Mother Marianne worked late into the night trimming hats with crepe and making black sashes for the girls to wear to Father Damien's funeral to show their respect. Mele Meheula, Pohaku Melemai and Malie Kauluwela , who would all live long enough to be witnesses for the Cause of Father Damien, went to the funeral the next day, together with the other girls from the Bishop Home. Pohaku Melemai and Malie Kauluwela, who were only 12 when they came to Kalaupapa with the Sisters in 1888, vividly remembered 50 years later how they wore white dresses with black sashes.

Father Wendelin described the funeral procession held on April 16 for his "beloved *confrere*."

> *First came the cross-bearer, then the singers and the members of a Confraternity, then the Sisters with the women and girls, and after them the coffin . . . Behind the coffin walked the officiating priest, accompanied by Father Conrady and the acolytes, followed by the Brothers with the boys and men.*[124]

Father Damien's funeral procession, Kalawao. *Detail of photo by Dr. S.B. Swift, Damien Museum Archives*

In accordance with his wishes, Father Damien was buried facing in the direction of the altar in his church, under the Pandanus tree where he first slept when he arrived at Kalawao.

Joseph Manu, Mele Meheula, Malie Kauluwela, and Pohaku Melemai were present at Father Damien's funeral and also when his body was exhumed in 1936. Two years later, they gave witness testimony for the Cause of Father Damien along with David Kamahana and David Ilihia. Remembering back half a century to 1888 and 1889, when they knew Father Damien, these most important witnesses to history recalled his great love for God and for the people of Kalaupapa, his prayerfulness, his humility, his patience, his simplicity, his strength of character and his sense of justice. Joseph Manu recalled: "He was really a saint . . . This is a feeling he always gave me."

Alice Cambra, Helen Kaai, and Mele Meheula make wreaths for Father Damien the day before his body was removed from Kalawao and returned to Belgium. *Courtesy Sister Roseanne La Manche*

David Kamahana recalled the day that Father Damien's body was removed from Kalawao:

I felt great pain when the authorities took the remains. Out of respect and the love I felt for Father Damien, I followed the funeral carriage up to the last moment, even if others went in front of it.

I love Father Damien . . . I think of him as my North Star
-- He guides me.

Dignity is not something that others can give to you.   It is
something inherent in each of us.   Recognizing the dignity
inherent in every human being is the beginning of human
rights.[125]

Bernard Ka`owakaokalani Punikai`a, composer, musician and
human rights advocate, who was separated from his mother at
the age of six and sent to Kalaupapa in 1942 at age eleven

Epilogue

Statue of Father Damien, Hawaii State Capitol. *Photo by Henry Law*

The Hawaii State motto, generally attributed to King Kamehameha III (1814 - 1854), is displayed on a plaque that hangs in front of the Hawaii State Capitol in Honolulu. The motto -- *Ua mau ke ea o ka aina i ka pono,* The life of the land is perpetuated in righteousness -- reflects a strong belief in justice and doing that which is right. Beneath the plaque stands a statue of Father Damien. In 1965, the Hawaii State Legislature designated King Kamehameha I and Father Damien as Hawaii's two "eminent and illustrious leaders worthy of commemoration in Statuary Hall" in the United States Capitol.[126] Identical statues of Father Damien were then placed in Washington, D.C. and Honolulu. Not only did this officially recognize the significant impact that the history of leprosy has had on Hawaii, but Father Damien's presence serves as a constant reminder of the need for justice and accountability on the part of those who make the laws that so deeply affect the lives of the people.

Father Damien kept a notebook at Kalawao in which he jotted down thoughts for his sermons. In these notes are several references to justice. In quoting St. Paul's Letter to the Romans, he wrote: "I am not ashamed of the Gospel . . . For the justice of God is revealed therein, from faith unto faith, as it is written. The just man liveth by faith."[127] Father Damien's 16 years at Kalawao were a profound expression of his sense of justice, his determination to do that which was right, and his strong belief in the innate dignity and worth of every human being.

It is now 120 years since Father Damien died amongst his friends at Kalawao. A cure for leprosy was discovered in 1941. In 1981, an extremely effective Multi-Drug Therapy was developed and, since that time, some 15 million people have been cured. However, an equal number of people, together with their family members, continue to face widespread discrimination because they once had this disease.

In the 21st century, the challenges surounding leprosy are related to the realization of identity, equality, justice, and human rights. Around the world, individuals long cured of leprosy continue to be denied basic rights outlined in the Universal Declaration of Human Rights, including: The right to home, the right to family, the right to work, the right to education, the right to nationality, the right to a standard of living adequate for health and well-being, the right to be free from degrading treatment, and the right to full development of personality.

Individuals whose lives have been challenged by leprosy are increasingly exerting their right to full and equal participation in all matters pertaining to their own lives and to their history. Until individuals affected by this disease fully regain their rightful place in their homes, communities, countries, and in their histories, leprosy will remain an essential challenge and a vital component in the international discussion of human rights and responsibilities.

In the context of leprosy as a human rights issue, the legacy of Father Damien, Mother Marianne, Queen Kapiolani, King Kalakaua, Queen Liliuokalani, Jonathan Napela, Ambrose Hutchison, and other important figures in Kalaupapa's history, is most relevant. Of vital importance is the example of so many Hawaiian families, who chose to respond to leprosy with great love rather than fear and, in so doing, resisted isolation policies that sought to separate and exclude.

As Father Damien stands watch over the international discussion of leprosy and human rights as it reaches the highest levels of government, one can almost hear the voices of the boys of Kalawao singing the song that they composed for their friend:

Here is Damien,

Our father,

His eyes are like the first glimmer of dawn,

Clear and sparkling

Upon seeing him, fond memories come to mind.

We are all like a family,

With one father,

Goodbye to you, goodbye to each of us,

May you return with aloha.

God be praised

The all-powerful parent

In the high heavens, and

Bringing peace to people

On earth who desire righteousness . . .

School children visit the Father Damien statue that stands in front of the Hawaii State Capitol. *Photo by A. Law*

Father Damien's grave at Kalawao. *Photo by Henry Law*

Acknowledgements

Kuulei Bell, Kalaupapa resident and first President of Ka `Ohana O Kalaupapa.

Paul Harada (left) and Makia Malo (right) at a Ka `Ohana O Kalaupapa meeting at Kalaupapa. *Photos by Wayne Levin*

Our heartfelt thanks goes to the current residents of Kalaupapa, and so many who are no longer with us, who have educated and inspired us over the years through their powerful words and generosity of spirit.

This book would not be in existence without the assistance of Patrick Boland who, over the decades, has consistently brought materials to our attention, particularly those related to Father Damien's relationship with the Hawaiian people.

We are especially grateful to the Congregation of the Sacred Hearts and their Archives in Louvain, Rome and Hawaii, for preserving the words and legacy of the people of Kalaupapa, through witness testimonies, letters and the memoirs of Ambrose Hutchison. We thank the family of Ambrose Hutchison, especially Robert Hutchison, for their insights into this most significant figure in Kalaupapa's history.

The Blessed Marianne Cope Museum and Archives in Syracuse, New York, is one of the best archives relating to Kalaupapa's history in the world. Our ongoing gratitude goes to Sister Mary Laurence Hanley for sharing her knowledge with regard to the information in this vast collection of documents, photographs, and artifacts. We also thank Sister Grace Anne Dillenschneider, Sister Pat Burkard, and Sister Roseanne La Manche for their assistance as well as all of the Sisters of St. Francis for their ongoing presence at Kalaupapa and their role in preserving this most important history.

We are continually grateful to Susan Shaner, Luella Kurkjian, Jason Achiu, and the staff of the Hawai`i State Archives for their assistance and support in so many ways over more than 30 years. We thank Joan Hori at Hamilton Library, University of Hawai`i Manoa, for her research assistance. For special help with photographs, we thank Barbara Dunn and the Hawaiian Historical Society; Leah Pualaha`ole Caldeira, Cynthia Engle, and the Bishop Museum Archives; Leslie Belais and the Wisconsin Historical Society; and Matt Kester and the BYU-Hawai`i Archives. In addition, we thank Professor Omer Steeno for sharing his knowledge of Dr. Eduard Arning and the photographs he took in the 1880's. We are also grateful to Frances Trotter Bell for sharing her collection of early photographs of Kalaupapa.

Over the years, Father Joseph Hendriks, Irene Letoto, and the Damien Museum have willingly shared their wealth of information and photographs related to Kalaupapa. We thank them and are also grateful to Brother Louis Leisen and Father Joseph Julliotte for taking many of those photographs. We appreciate the support of the Hawaii State Library for the Blind, Kalaupapa National Historical Park, and the Arizona Memorial Museum Association, who recognized early on the importance of recording oral history with the people of Kalaupapa.

We are most appreciative of the support of Dr. Ben Young and the Native Hawaiian Center of Excellence who have, over many years, supported the research that has enabled us to include documents originally written in Hawaiian in this and other publications. We are also grateful to Sol Kaho`ohalahala and David and Thomas Groom for their most important contribution to this effort. We thank Howard Crouch, Betty Campbell, and the Damien-Dutton Society for their friendship and willingness to support requests for help with unanticipated needs related to this book and other efforts.

We thank Frances N. Frazier, Carol L. Silva, Jason Achiu, and Kiki Mookini for their ongoing assistance with the translation of materials from Hawaiian to English. We also thank Colette Higgins for sharing her insights into Queen Kapiolani. We are most grateful to Felicita Veluri and Dr. Sunil Deepak of the Italian Association Amici di Raoul Follereau for their assistance in translating the witness testimonies from Italian to English. We also thank Mary and John Gaudet for their decades of support and for sharing their translation of Bishop Maigret's Diary.

Thanks to Valerie Monson for all of her efforts to preserve Kalaupapa's history and her willingness to always lend an ear to new ideas and for introducing us to the wisdom of Kaili`ohe Kame`ekua. Our special thanks go to Johnna Willis Thomas, who enabled us to incorporate the wisdom of Kaili`ohe Kame`ekua in this book by permitting us to quote excerpts from *Tales from the Night Rainbow*.

We are grateful to Emma Kamahana Dickerson for sharing her recollections of her father, David Kamahana, and to her family for their commitment to seeing that the Kamahana family legacy is preserved at Kalaupapa. We thank Kelli Wicke Davis for sharing the photograph of her relative, William Clark, and Emmet Cheeley for introducing us to Kelli. We also thank Chris and David Mahelona for sharing their research on Jonathan Napela.

We thank Pennie Moblo for sharing her detailed research into Kalaupapa's history. We are also greatly appreciative of the research done by Noenoe Silva and Pualeilani Fernandez to identify all of the references to Kalaupapa's history in the Hawaiian language newspapers.

Over the years, Wayne Levin has consistently photographed the people and events related to Kalaupapa. We thank him for his talent and willingness to always be present to record this most important history. We also thank the inimitable Gene Balbach for his creative efforts to ensure that the history of Kalaupapa's people would not be forgotten.

We thank Mary O'Friel for her invaluable assistance with editing and other support; and Gail Lohr for her insights. We also thank Patrick Downes, Editor of the *Hawaii Catholic Herald*, for his assistance with editing, promotion and distribution of the book. We thank Sanford Kame`ekua and Virginia Murison Whitcomb for help in communication.

We thank our family for their ongoing support and especially our daughter, Lian, for her wisdom and patience.

Finally, we thank Bishop Larry Silva for his Foreword and encouragement, and for opening the doors of his family history to ensure that his relatives, John Santos and Minnie Santos Arruda, will be part of the permanent history of Kalaupapa and, consequently, the history of, in his words, "our beloved Father Damien."

Notes

1. Pali Jae Lee and Koko Willis, *Tales from the Night Rainbow, Moʻolelo o na Pō Mākole: The Story of a Woman, a People, and an Island*, Revised and English Edition (Honolulu: Night Rainbow Publishing Company, 1990) 17. Quoted with permission from Johnna Willis Thomas

2. All quotes from Joseph Manu come from: *Beatificationis et Canonizationis Servi Dei Damiani De Veuster, Missionarii, Sacerdotis Professi, Congregationis SS. Cordium Jesu et Mariae (Picpus), Positio Super Virtutibus* (Rome: Guerra & Belli, 1966). Translated from Italian by Felicita Veluri and Dr. Sunil Deepak

3. Lee and Willis, xiii and 61-62.

4. All quotes from Ambrose Hutchison come from the unpublished, handwritten manuscript: "In Memoria of Reverend Father Damien J. De Veuster and Other Priests," Archives of the Congregation of the Sacred Hearts, Louvain, and Hawaiʻi State Archives (partial manuscript).

5. All quotes from Pohaku Melemai and Mary (Malie) Kauluwela Keliikaapuni come from: *Beatificationis et Canonizationis Servi Dei Damiani De Veuster, Missionarii, Sacerdotis Professi, Congregationis SS. Cordium Jesu et Mariae (Picpus), Positio Super Virtutibus* (Rome: Guerra & Belli, 1966). Translated from Italian by Felicita Veluri and Dr. Sunil Deepak

6. All quotes from Mele Meheula come from: *Beatificationis et Canonizationis Servi Dei Damiani De Veuster, Missionarii, Sacerdotis Professi, Congregationis SS. Cordium Jesu et Mariae (Picpus), Positio Super Virtutibus* (Rome: Guerra & Belli, 1966). Translated from Italian by Felicita Veluri and Dr. Sunil Deepak

7. Interview with Emma Kamahana Dickerson by Anwei Law, 17 November 2008.

8. Francisco Camacho to Father Damien, 16 December 1888, Damien Museum Archives.

9. Rev. Joseph Damien, "A Personal Experience"; A.A. Mouritz, *The Path of the Destroyer* (Honolulu: Honolulu Star-Bulletin, Ltd., 1916) 222.

10. Record of Inmates at Kalaupapa, 1866-1899 (1903), Hawaiʻi State Archives. [Note: A few individuals listed on this Admission Register were *kokua* or *kamaaina* who did not actually have leprosy]

11. R.W. Meyer to Dr. F.W. Hutchison, 22 January 1866; J.D. Kahauliko to T.C. Heuck, 24 March 1866, Incoming Letters of the Board of Health, Hawaiʻi State Archives. Translated from Hawaiian by Carol L. Silva

12. Personal communication, William K. Malo, 2006.

13. Report of the Board of Health to the Legislative Assembly of 1868, *Leprosy in Hawaii* (Honolulu, 1886) 44, 48.

14. J.H. Napela to E.O. Hall, 23 October 1873, Incoming Letters of the Board of Health, Hawaiʻi State Archives. Translated from Hawaiian by Frances N. Frazier

15. Mouritz, 222.

16. Mouritz, 222.

17. Father Damien to his parents, 30 October 1863; Father Pamphile De Veuster (Editor), *Life and Letters of Father Damien* (London: The Catholic Truth Society, 1889) 49.

18. Father Damien to Father Pamphile, 23 August 1864; Pamphile, 60-61.

19. Father Damien to his parents, 12 October 1869; Pamphile, 73.

20. Father Damien to Dr. F. W. Hutchison, 22 October 1870, Incoming Letters of the Board of Health, Hawai`i State Archives. [Note: This letter no longer seems to be a part of this file, but was referred to in research conducted by Pennie Moblo for her dissertation, "Defamation by Disease: Leprosy, Myth and Ideology in Nineteenth Century Hawaii," University of Hawaii, 1996]

21. Vital Jourdain, SS.CC., *The Heart of Father Damien* (Milwaukee: The Bruce Publishing Company, 1955) 98.

22. Michael Kaloa to Rev. Father Damien, 17 October 1881, Translated from Hawaiian, Damien Museum Archives. [Note: The contents of this letter suggest that it was written in 1888 rather than 1881]

23. Jourdain, 96.

24. Record of Inmates at Kalaupapa, 1866-1899, Hawai`i State Archives.

25. Bishop Maigret's Diary, Entry for 10 May 1873, Transcribed and Translated from French by Mary and John Gaudet, Courtesy Mary and John Gaudet.

26. Isabella L. Bird, *Six Months in the Sandwich Islands* (Honolulu: Mutual Publishing, 1998) 142. [Note: Isabella Bird wrote about Upa in 1873]

27. Father Damien to Father Modeste, 12 May 1873, Archives of the Congregation of the Sacred Hearts, Hawaii.

28. Record of Inmates at Kalaupapa, 1866-1899, Hawai`i State Archives. [Note: A total of 477 people were sent to Kalawao in 1873, of whom 466 were identified as Hawaiian]

29. R.W. Meyer to Dr. George Trousseau, 31 March 1873, Incoming Letters of the Board of Health, Hawai`i State Archives.

30. Mouritz, 211.

31. Mouritz, 212.

32. Joseph Dutton statement regarding Father Damien, February, 1890; Revised 15 October 1903, Archives of the Congregation of the Sacred Hearts, Louvain.

33. Interview with Richard Marks by Anwei Skinsnes, 14 June 1985.

34. Father Damien to his mother, brothers and sisters, 8 December 1874; Pamphile, 99.

35. Peter Kaeo to Queen Emma, 9 December 1873, Manuscript Collection Emma Kaleleonalani, Queen of the Hawaiian Islands, Folders 16-20, Hawai`i State Archives; Also, Alfons Korn (Editor), *News from Molokai: Letters Between Peter Kaeo & Queen Emma, 1873-1876* (Honolulu: The University Press of Hawai`i, 1976), 153. [Note: Peter Kaeo's letters were written in English and his original spelling and punctuation are retained]

36. Peter Kaeo to Queen Emma, 1 July 1873, Hawa`i State Archives; Also Korn, 9.

37. Peter Kaeo to Queen Emma, 31 August 1873, Hawai`i State Archives; Also Korn, 80.

38. Peter Kaeo to Queen Emma, 1 October 1873, Hawai`i State Archives; Also Korn, 123.

39. Mouritz, 218.

40. Robert C. Lydecker, *Roster, Legislatures of Hawaii, 1841-1918* (Honolulu: The Hawaiian Gazette Co., Ltd., 1918) 103.

41. Jonathan Napela to Edwin O. Hall, 20 April 1873, Incoming Letters of the Board of Health, Hawai`i State Archives. Translated from Hawaiian by Jason Achiu

42. Mouritz, 227-228.

43. Mouritz, 227-228.

44. *Pacific Commercial Advertiser*, 18 April 1874.

45. Petition from Kalaupapa, Molokai, to the Hawaiian Legislature, 3 June 1874, Hawai`i State Archives. Translated from Hawaiian by Jason Achiu

46. Peter Kaeo to Queen Emma, 22 November 1874, Hawai`i State Archives; Also Korn, 262.

47. Mouritz, 217.

48. Damien J. De Veuster to his mother and brothers, April, 1877; Pamphile, 113

49. Report of the Special Sanitary Committee, *Pacific Commercial Advertiser*, 8 June 1878.

50. Jourdain, 203.

51. Mouritz, 226.

52. All quotes from David Ilihia come from: *Beatificationis et Canonizationis Servi Dei Damiani De Veuster, Missionarii, Sacerdotis Professi, Congregationis SS. Cordium Jesu et Mariae (Picpus), Positio Super Virtutibus* (Rome: Guerra & Belli, 1966). Translated from Italian by Felicita Veluri and Dr. Sunil Deepak

53. N.D. Kahoana to Father Damien, 1 August 1887, Translated from Hawaiian, Damien Museum Archives. [Note: The spelling of Hawaiian names in this and other letters from this collection, i.e., Notes 53-55 and 63-68, are difficult to discern with certainty since only the translation, and not the original, is available]

54. M. Leo to Father Damien, 23 April 1884, Translated from Hawaiian, Damien Museum Archives.

55. P. Nauka, Pelekunu Valley, to Father Damien, 29 September 1884, Translated from Hawaiian, Damien Museum Archives.

56. John Puaina Wilmington, Statement about Father Damien recorded by Father Martin Dornbush, Damien Museum Archives.

57. Unless otherwise indicated, all information in this chapter comes from: Pali Jae Lee and Koko Willis, *Tales from the Night Rainbow, Mo'olelo o na Pō Mākole: The Story of a Woman, a People, and an Island*, Revised and English Edition (Honolulu: Night Rainbow Publishing Company, 1990). Quoted with permission from Johnna Willis Thomas

58. "Bowl of Light: A Counseling Tool," Website of the Barbara Sinatra Children's Center; Website of Hinduism Today; Website of the Inter-faith Roundtable of Kauai.

59. Record of Inmates at Kalaupapa, 1866-1899, Hawai'i State Archives.

60. Mouritz, 225-226

61. Mouritz, 207-208.

62. All quotes from David Kamahana come from: *Beatificationis et Canonizationis Servi Dei Damiani De Veuster, Missionarii, Sacerdotis Professi, Congregationis SS. Cordium Jesu et Mariae (Picpus), Positio Super Virtutibus* (Rome: Guerra & Belli, 1966). Translated from Italian by Felicita Veluri and Dr. Sunil Deepak

63. John from Pauoa to Father Damien, 18 February 1889, Translated from Hawaiian, Damien Museum Archives.

64. Cecelia Haliimaile, Honolulu, to Father Damien, 20 February 1888, Translated from Hawaiian, Damien Museum Archives.

65. S.H. Mookapu to Father Damien, 6 August 1888, Translated from Hawaiian, Damien Museum Archives.

66. Victoria to Father Damien, 9 April 1880, Translated from Hawaiian, Damien Museum Archives.

67. D.K.M. Keohokalolo, Kakaako, to Father Damien, 23 July 1883, Translated from Hawaiian, Damien Museum Archives.

68. Mr. S. Hoopii, Lahaina, to Rev. Father J. Damien, 17 August 1885, Translated from Hawaiian, Damien Museum Archives.

69. Father Damien to M. Cullen, Esq., 29 August 1881, Damien Museum Archives.

70. Kuaana to Father Damien, 10 September 1887, Translated from Hawaiian, Damien Museum Archives. [Note: *Lauhala* hats are woven from pandanus leaves]

71. Jourdain, 200.

72.   Jourdain, 203.

73   Diary of Bishop Maigret, Entry for 10 June 1873, Transcribed and Translated from French by Mary and John Gaudet, Courtesy Mary and John Gaudet.

74.   Jourdain, 204.

75.   *Hawaiian Gazette*, 21 September 1881.

76.   Gavan Daws, *Holy Man* (New York: Harper and Row, Publishers, 1973) 100.

77.   Princess Liliuokalani to Father Damien, 1881; Pamphile, 126.

78.   Father Damien to Princess Liliuokalani, 1 October 1881, Records of the Foreign Office & Executive, Hawai`i State Archives.

79.   Father Damien to Father Pamphile, 8 December 1881; Pamphile, 122.

80.   Jourdain, 201-202.

81.   Queen Kapiolani to Father Damien, 11 August 1884, Translated from Hawaiian, Damien Museum Archives.

82.   "Report of Her Majesty Queen Kapiolani's Visit to Molokai by H.R.H. Princess Liliuokalani, July, 1884"; Mouritz, 295-296.

83.   Father Damien to Queen Kapiolani, 6 August 1884; Jourdain, 404. Translated from Hawaiian by Therese Malani [Note: Miss Malani characterized Father Damien's Hawaiian as "flawless and in classical style"]

84.   Queen Kapiolani to Father Damien, 11 August 1884, Translated from Hawaiian, Damien Museum Archives.

85.   Queen Kapiolani to Father Damien, 8 October 1884, Translated from Hawaiian, Damien Museum Archives.

86.   Program, "The Dedication of the Kapiolani Home," Blessed Marianne Cope Museum and Archives.

87.   *Pacific Commercial Advertiser*, 8 March 1884.

88.   "A Royal Visit," *Pacific Commercial Advertiser*, 25 May 1884.

89.   Daws, 162.

90.   Father Damien to Bishop Koeckemann; Pamphile, 133.

91.   Dr. Arthur Mouritz, *Testimony for the Cause of the Servant of God Joseph Damien De Veuster, 1938*, Archives of the Archbishop of Mechelen, Belgium.

92.   Father Leonor Fouesnel to Father Damien, 8 February 1886; Jourdain, 337.

93. Translation of letter from Father Damien to Bishop Hermann Koeckemann, 16 June 1886, Blessed Marianne Cope Museum and Archives. [Original letter in the Archives of the Congregation of the Sacred Hearts, Rome]

94. Translation of letter from Dr. Arthur Mouritz to Bishop Hermann Koeckemann, 5 June 1886, Blessed Marianne Cope Museum and Archives. [Original letter in the Archives of the Congregation of the Sacred Hearts, Rome. Note: The existence of translations for letters that were probably originally written in English may reflect the fact that documents were translated into other languages, such as French, Italian, and Latin, when they were submitted as part of the research for the Cause of Father Damien]

95. Translation of letter from R.W. Meyer to Father Damien, 8 July 1886, Blessed Marianne Cope Museum and Archives. [Original letter in the Archives of the Congregation of the Sacred Hearts, Rome]

96. Jacob Adler and Gwynn Barrett (Editors), *The Diaries of Walter Murray Gibson, 1886, 1887* (Honolulu: The University Press of Hawaii, 1973) 58.

97. Sister Mary Laurence Hanley, O.S.F. and O.A Bushnell, *Pilgrimage and Exile, Mother Marianne of Molokai* (Honolulu: University of Hawai`i Press, 1991) 249.

98. Mouritz, 208.

99. Joseph Dutton to Father Daniel Hudson, 20 November 1891, University of Notre Dame Archives.

100. Mouritz, *Testimony, 1938.*

101. Howard D. Case (Editor), *Joseph Dutton, His Memoirs* (Honolulu: The Honolulu Star-Bulletin Press, 1931) 48-49.

102. Mouritz, 285.

103. Father Damien to Father Daniel Hudson, 23 November 1886, University of Notre Dame Archives.

104. Joseph Dutton memo to Father Reginald, 1 January 1914, University of Notre Dame Archives.

105. Father Damien to Fred Hayselden, 15 September 1886, Masonic Public Library Hawaii.

106. Father Damien to Rev. H.B. Chapman, January, 1887, Archives of the Congregation of the Sacred Hearts, Louvain.

107. Joseph Dutton to Father Daniel Hudson, 25 January 1887, University of Notre Dame Archives.

108. Translation of letter from Bishop Hermann Koeckemann to Father M. Bousquet, 15 February 1887, Blessed Marianne Cope Museum and Archives. [Original letter in Archives of the Congregation of the Sacred Hearts, Rome]

109. Translation of letter from Father Leonor Fouesnel to Father M. Bousquet, 8 February 1887, Blessed Marianne Cope Museum and Archives. [Original letter in the Archives of the Congregation of the Sacred Hearts, Rome]

110. Translation of letter from Father Leonor Fouesnel to Father Damien, 21 April 1887, Blessed Marianne Cope Museum and Archives. [Original letter in the Archives of the Congregation of the Sacred Hearts, Rome]

111. Jourdain, 290.

112. Mouritz, *Testimony, 1938.*

113. Father Damien to Father Daniel Hudson, 8 August 1888, University of Notre Dame Archives.

114. "Na Palapala," Letter to the Editor from Thomas K. Nakanaela, *Ke Aloha Aina*, 14 March 1897. Translated from Hawaiian by Jason Achiu

115. Record of Inmates at Kalaupapa, 1866-1899, Hawai`i State Archives.

116. *Origin and History of St. Elizabeth's Convent, Kalaupapa, Molokai, 1888,* Entry by Father Matthias Limburg, SS.CC., 13 November 1888, Blessed Marianne Cope Museum and Archives.

117. Dr. N.B. Emerson to the Committee, 23 December 1888, Blessed Marianne Cope Museum and Archives.

118. Francisco Camacho to Father Damien, 16 December 1888, Damien Museum Archives.

119. All quotations from Edward Clifford are from: *Edward Clifford, Father Damien, A Journey from Cashmere to His Home in Hawaii* (London: MacMillan and Company, 1889).

120. Father Damien to Father Pamphile, 19 February 1889; Pamphile, 146.

121. Letter of Father Wendelin, 17 April 1889; Pamphile, 147-148.

122. Letter of Father Wendelin, 17 April 1889; Pamphile, 149.

123. The Journal of Sister Leopoldina Burns, Blessed Marianne Cope Museum and Archives.

124. Letter of Father Wendelin, 17 April 1889; Pamphile, 150.

125. Personal communication, Bernard K. Punikai`a, 1999.

126. *The King Kamehameha I and Father Damien Memorial Statues*, Senate Document Number 91-54 (Washington: U.S. Government Printing House, 1970).

127. Father Damien Notebook and Sermons, Damien Museum Archives.

Bibliography

Information in this book comes from manuscript and/or photograph collections in the following archives and libraries: The Archives of the Congregation of the Sacred Hearts in Rome, Louvain, and Hawaii (copies of letters and documents from these collections, obtained by Gavan Daws as part of his research, are located on microfilm at Hamilton Library, University of Hawai`i Manoa); The Blessed Marianne Cope Museum and Archives; The Damien Museum Archives; The Hawai`i State Archives; The Hawaiian Historical Society; The Bishop Museum Archives; The Wisconsin Historical Society; and The University of Notre Dame Archives. In addition, the following books have also been cited to varying degrees.

Adler, Jacob, and Gwynn Barrett, Editors. *The Diaries of Walter Murray Gibson, 1886, 1887*. Honolulu: The University Press of Hawaii, 1973.

Beatificationis et Canonizationis Servi Dei Damiani De Veuster, Missionarii, Sacerdotis Professi, Congregationis SS. Cordium Jesu et Mariae (Picpus), Positio Super Virtutibus. Rome: Guerra & Belli, 1966.

Bird, Isabella L. *Six Months in the Sandwich Islands*. Honolulu: Mutual Publishing, 1998.

Case, Howard D., Editor. *Joseph Dutton, His Memoirs*. Honolulu: The Honolulu Star-Bulletin Press, 1931.

Clifford, Edward. *Father Damien, A Journey from Cashmere to His Home in Hawaii*. London: MacMillan and Company, 1889.

Daws, Gavan. *Holy Man*. New York: Harper and Row, Publishers, 1973.

De Veuster, Father Pamphile, Editor. *Life and Letters of Father Damien*. London: The Catholic Truth Society, 1889.

Hanley, Sister Mary, O.S.F., and O.A Bushnell. *Pilgrimage and Exile, Mother Marianne of Molokai*. Honolulu: University of Hawai`i Press, 1991.

Jourdain, Vital, SS.CC. *The Heart of Father Damien*. Translated by Rev. Francis Larkin, SS.CC. and Charles Davenport. Milwaukee: The Bruce Publishing Company, 1955.

Korn, Alfons, Editor. *News from Molokai: Letters Between Peter Kaeo & Queen Emma, 1873-1876*. Honolulu: The University Press of Hawaii, 1976.

Lee, Pali Jae, and Koko Willis. *Tales from the Night Rainbow, Mo`olelo o na Pō Mākole: The Story of a Woman, a People, and an Island*, Revised and English Edition. Honolulu: Night Rainbow Publishing Company, 1990.

Lydecker, Robert C. *Roster, Legislatures of Hawaii, 1841-1918*. Honolulu: The Hawaiian Gazette Co. Ltd., 1918.

Mouritz, A.A. *The Path of the Destroyer*. Honolulu: Honolulu Star-Bulletin, Ltd., 1916.

About the Authors

Anwei Skinsnes Law first visited Kalaupapa in 1968 at the age of 16. Over the last 40 years, she has extensively researched the history of leprosy in Hawaii and conducted over 200 hours of oral history interviews with the residents of Kalaupapa. In 1982, she received a Master's Degree in Public Health from the University of Hawai`i School of Public Health. In 1989, she published *Kalaupapa: A Portrait* with photographer Wayne Levin. She is also the author of *The Great Flood: Johnstown, Pennsylvania, 1889.* Ms. Law coordinated the Oral History Project of the ILA Global Project on the History of Leprosy, in which interviews were conducted with people from 35 countries, speaking in more than 20 languages. She is currently working on a detailed history of Kalaupapa entitled: *"Ka Hokuwelowelo: A Collective Memory of Kalaupapa"* to be published by The University of Hawai`i Press. She is the International Coordinator of IDEA and a founding member of Ka `Ohana O Kalaupapa.

Henry G. Law was an Historical Architect and Park Manager with the U. S. National Park Service for more than 26 years. He has also been a photographer for more than 35 years. He first went to Kalaupapa in 1977 as part of the National Park Service planning team to conduct the new area study for Kalaupapa prior to it being designated a National Historical Park in 1980. In 1982, he became the first National Park Service employee at Kalaupapa and in 1984 became the first superintendent of Kalaupapa National Historical Park. Mr. Law currently works with IDEA and is a founding member of Ka`Ohana O Kalaupapa.

IDEA, the International Association for Integration, Dignity and Economic Advancement, is the largest international advocacy organization by and for individuals who have personally faced the challenges of leprosy, also known as Hansen's disease. As a Non-Governmental Organization in Special Consultative Status with the Economic and Social Council of the United Nations, IDEA actively works to ensure the human rights of every individual whose life has been affected by leprosy. Through its publications, workshops, international conferences and the IDEA Center for the Voices of Humanity, IDEA works to provide a forum for the voices of people around the world whose lives have been challenged by leprosy. Through the use of positive images and dignified terminology, IDEA seeks to replace old images with modern day realities. In 2003, IDEA launched a Global Campaign to Eliminate the Stigma Associated with Leprosy. Ensuring that people are afforded their rightful place in history and the restoration of family ties are two important components of this Campaign.

To learn more about IDEA, issues related to leprosy and human rights, and the current situation with regard to leprosy, please go to: www.idealeprosydignity.org.

To learn more about Ka`Ohana O Kalaupapa, an organization composed of current Kalaupapa residents, family members, and others interested in preserving the history and legacy of the people of Kalaupapa, please go to: www.kalaupapaohana.org.